**WALKING BETWEEN
SLUMS and
SKYSCRAPERS**

Hong Kong University Press thanks Xu Bing for writing the Press's name in his Square Word Calligraphy for the covers of its books. For further information, see p. iv.

In memory of

my father, Huang Ting-rong,
Professor Michael Sprinker,
and
Dongdong

Walking Between Slums and Skyscrapers

Illusions of Open Space in Hong Kong, Tokyo, and Shanghai

Tsung-yi Michelle Huang

香港大學出版社
Hong Kong University Press

Hong Kong University Press
14/F Hing Wai Centre
7 Tin Wan Praya Road
Aberdeen
Hong Kong

© Hong Kong University Press 2004

ISBN 962 209 635 2 (Hardback)
ISBN 962 209 636 0 (Paperback)

All rights reserved. No part of this publication may be reproduced or transmitted, in any form or by any means, electronic or mechanical, including photocopy, recording, or any information storage or retrieval system, without prior permission in writing from the publisher.

British Library Cataloguing-in-Publication Data
A catalogue record for this book is available from the British Library.

Secure On-line Ordering
http://www.hkupress.org

Printed and bound by Caritas Printing Training Centre, Hong Kong, China

Hong Kong University Press is honoured that Xu Bing, whose art explores the complex themes of language across cultures, has written the Press's name in his Square Word Calligraphy. This signals our commitment to cross-cultural thinking and the distinctive nature of our English-language books published in China.

"At first glance, Square Word Calligraphy appears to be nothing more unusual than Chinese characters, but in fact it is a new way of rendering English words in the format of a square so they resemble Chinese characters. Chinese viewers expect to be able to read Square Word Calligraphy but cannot. Western viewers, however are surprised to find they can read it. Delight erupts when meaning is unexpectedly revealed."

— Britta Erickson, *The Art of Xu Bing*

Contents

Acknowledgements ix

Introduction 1
Walking in the Global City: Whose Open Space Is It?

PART ONE
Hong Kong Blue: Where Have All the *Flâneurs* Gone? 13
Walking in Between Eternal Dual Compression

Chapter 1
Hong Kong: A Nodal Point of Dual Compression 15
— From British Empire Colony to Disney Kingdom Outpost
— Disneyfication of the City: The Global Compression
— Not Just the Tourists: Local Compression and Public Housing in Hong Kong

Chapter 2
Chungking Express: Walking With a Map of Desire in the 31
Mirage of the Global City
— Space of Fantasy/Map of Desire
— Lost in a Big City: Global Space as a Mirage
— *Femme Fatale* or Disoriented Dupe? The Walker With a Blonde Wig and a Wrong Map
— Multilingual as Global: The Talking *Flâneur* Looking for a Return Gaze

- Airport/Global Space/Women: The Self-pity *Flâneur*
- California Dreaming in Hong Kong: The Female *Flâneur* as a Mirror

Chapter 3
Between Representations of Space and Representational Spaces: 49
Flâneurie With the Camera's Eye
- Shock Defense and the Director-*Flâneur*'s Authentic Map of Hong Kong
- Shock Defense and *Flâneur*'s Resistance to Modernization

PART TWO
Between Global Flows and Carnal Flows: Walking in Tokyo — 57

Chapter 4
Mimesis: The Violence of Space — 63
- Abstract Space *Par Excellence*: Global/Fragmentary Space of Tokyo
- Global City Tokyo: An Official Story
- All the Glittering Buildings: You Are What You See

Chapter 5
From Mimesis to Mimicry: Memory, Subjectivity, and Space — 77
- Salaryman or Iron Man? *Tetsuo: The Iron Man* and *Tetsuo II: Body Hammer*
- Of a Man and a Building: *Tokyo Fist*
- Walking as a Salaryman: What's Wrong With It?

PART THREE
Mirror, Mirror, On the Wall: Walking in Shanghai, a Global City — 99
in the Making

Chapter 6
"Build it and They will Come": Transformation of Pudong Into a — 103
Copy of the Global City
- Global City Formation: What Can Go Wrong?

Chapter 7
From Alley Houses to High-rises: What Happened to the Lived Space? 111
— Mirror and Mirage: Whose Global City Is It?

Chapter 8
Sleeping Beauty Waking up to a New World of Capital: 119
Wang Anyi's Shanghai Stories
— Mirage of Old Shanghai: "Meitou" and *The Song of Unending Sorrow*
— Looking for Shanghai: Meandering on Foot in a Labyrinthian City of Mirrors

Coda 137

Bibliography 139

Notes 147

Index 167

Acknowledgements

The completion of this book would have been impossible without Mike Davis, Ban Wang, Beverly Haviland, Cliff Siskin and Krin Gabbard. I owe them a great deal for their astute criticism and intellectual stimulation. The Chiang Ching-kuo Foundation and United World Chinese Commercial Bank kindly granted me a fellowship in 2000 so that I was able to conduct my research in Shanghai and complete the last part of this project. I also want to thank the anonymous readers of my manuscript, the Acquisitions Editors at Hong Kong University Press, Ms. Mina Cerny Kuma and Ms. Delphine Yip, and particularly the Managing Editor of the Press, Mr. Dennis Cheung , for their invaluable comments and professional advice. Ms. Mary Padua and Mr. Yen-bin Chiou kindly offer photos for the first two parts of the book. Their generosity is deeply appreciated.

Three chapters of this book are revised versions of articles published earlier: "Hong Kong Blue: *Flâneurie* With the Camera's Eye in a Phantasmagoric Global City," published in *Journal of Narrative Theory,* 30, no. 3 (2000); "*Chungking Express*: Walking With a Map of Desire in the Mirage of the Global City," from *Quarterly Review of Film and Video,* 18, no. 2 (2001); and "*Tetsuo*: Salaryman or Iron Man?" posted on line in the special edition of Asian cinema review in *Scope* (2003). I thank the editors of these three journals for allowing me to reprint the essays in this book.

I thank friends at Stony Brook, Ching-ling Wo, Zhen Zhang, Xiaoning Lu, Yanmei Wei, Zhaohui Xiong, Stuart Kendall, Max Stakiewicz, Modhumita Roy, and Alessandra Moctezuma, for their company and comradeship. It was very lucky for me to get to know these brilliant souls. I am obliged to the Lemings, our best friends and great neighbors. Beatrice, Howell and Mary read most of this book and offered the most careful editorial advice. Several individuals in Taiwan also have helped me in different ways to complete the book: Dr. Ching-hsi Perng, Dr. Yao-fu Lin, Dr. Douglas Berman, Tony Chen, Vita Tong, Yaw-sheng Lin, Yuan-lin Hsieh, and Sai-mei Hu.

Most importantly, I want to thank my family for their support and encouragement all these years: my mom, my stepfather, my sisters Tsung-huei and Tsung-chieh, and my brother-in-law Yen-bin. I want them to know that it is their love that led me to where I am today. Special thanks go to my husband Chi-she, who walked me through these years with lots of love and patience. The numerous walks we took at Stony Brook, exchanging our ideas about what we were working on, now become the sweetest memories of our Long Island days. I have benefited enormously from his intellectual inspiration and insightful critique. In fact, this book is in many ways his baby as much as mine.

Finally, I would like to dedicate this book to my father, Ting-rong Huang, who passed away when I was ten, and to the late Dr. Michael Sprinker, who has been and will always be the thought that keeps me working hard both as a scholar and as a teacher.

Introduction
Walking in the Global City:
Whose Open Space Is It?

> Capitalism thereby builds and rebuilds a geography in its own image. It constructs a distinctive geographical landscape, a produced space of transport and communications, of infrastructures and territorial organizations, that facilitates capital accumulation during one phase of its history only to have to be torn down and reconfigured to make way for further accumulation at a later stage. If, therefore, the word "globalization" signifies anything about our recent historical geography, it is most likely to be a new phase of exactly this same underlying process of the capitalist production of space.
>
> David Harvey

> If there is a history of walking, then it too has come to a place where the road falls off, a place where there is no public space and the landscape is being paved over, where leisure is shrinking and being crushed under the anxiety to produce, where bodies are not in the world but only indoors in cars and buildings, and an apotheosis of speed makes those bodies seem anachronistic or feeble.
>
> Rebecca Solnit

I was writing the last part of this project when the horrors of the September 11 attacks shocked the world. New York City, the global city that serves as a role model for many metropolises in the world, suffered the most audacious terrorist attacks. The collapse of the World Trade Center, the landmark of the quintessential global city, urges us to rethink the monumental space as an emblem of invincible power and the problems entailed by globalization. It is noteworthy that the very globalization that gives rise to these monumental buildings also leads to their destruction: airplanes, a means and symbol of globalization, become a weapon in the hands of terrorists, who cross borders which were made permeable to facilitate global flows of information, travel, and capital. The capital flows that empower the monumental buildings can protect neither the steel and concrete of the skyscrapers nor the corporeality of those who inhabit the space. The fact that the global economy slowed down after the attacks further attests to the vulnerability of globalization, demonstrating what happens when "the center cannot hold." On the other hand, the tragedies, in a sense, mirror the dire consequences of the uneven development of globalization. The war between the US, the economic superpower, and Afghanistan, one of the most impoverished countries in the world, cannot be explained by merely another confrontation between Christianity and Islam or the good and the evil as simplified by George W. Bush.[1] It is also a clash between those who profit from capital flows and the marginalized others that relentlessly have been excluded from the process of globalization.

* * * * * *

Recurrent in its commercials, Microsoft emphasizes the slogan: "So we will ask it again: *Where do you want to go today?*" (emphasis original) The slogan exemplifies the ideology of open space enabled by globalization. Utilizing advanced technologies in the areas of communications and transportation, globalization in many ways seems to open up more possibilities in contemporary society, entailing such phenomena as deterritorialization, the decline of nation-state control, and decorporealization (abstraction of bodily experience).[2] Specifically, the utopia of globalization is a flexible, fluid, and mobile space, an open space that knows no boundaries. Just as the jumbo jet constantly reminds us of how modern transportation compresses the physical spaces and renders faraway places as close as one's backyard, the world wide web as part of the information revolution makes the world a virtual reality at one's fingertips.

One of the persistent concerns in this project is about the effects of globalization on our lived space of everyday life as witnessed in East Asian metropolises including Hong Kong, Tokyo, and Shanghai. To examine the ideology of the open space produced by globalization, it is essential to turn to cities. However mobile global capital can be, it requires concrete material spaces for production, administration, and consumption: metropolises are thus chosen for flexible accumulation (Sassen 1996: 207–9). Given the increasing importance of the megalopolises, we need to address the following questions: How does the production of the global city change the lived space of the local people? Is the global city an open space for all of the inhabitants as many of its promoters celebrate? Or do the new possibilities brought about by the global flows compose another version of the myth of emancipation? My object of study focuses on one important dimension of the interaction between urban inhabitants and the East Asian global cities, the politics of walking as a practice and metaphor.[3] I explore films and literary works that address the politics of walking because in global culture it is often on the ground of narrativization that walking and the ideology of open space ally. The artistic works I analyze include Hong Kong director Wong Kar-wai's film *Chungking Express*, Japanese director Shinya Tsukamoto's works *Tetsuo: The Iron Man*, *Tetsuo II: Body Hammer*, and *Tokyo Fist*, and Chinese novelist Wang Anyi's "Meitou," "Looking for Shanghai," and *The Song of Unending Sorrow*. I argue that walking in the global city reveals the contradiction between everyday life and globalization. It is through walking that one witnesses vividly the oscillation between the yearning evoked by the ideology of open space and the dejection caused by the compression of living space as a consequence of capital globalization.

In the history of walking we see a drastic shift in the modern time from roaming in the wild nature to promenading in the urban street. From the ancient Greeks to the last quarter of the twentieth century, from garden path to pastoral, from boulevard and arcade to a labyrinthine, kaleidoscopic metropolis constructed and constrained by technology and global capital, walking, as a simple physical act that allows us to move beyond the confines of the body, has been utilized as an important means of access to and construction of a liberating open space. Giving lectures while walking on a covered path in the garden, Aristotle and his peripatetic school used walking as a way to prepare the thinking subjects for acquiring truth, which points to freedom. The intricate relationship between walking in Nature and the ideology of open space takes another form in Romantic poetry. For example, in Wordsworth's poems, pacing around the countryside, the poet finds a path to himself, to Nature, to people, and to everyday life. Here an important connotation of the poet's walking is its intimation of liberation in democratically open Nature. It is noteworthy, however, that the long tradition of walking as a means to spatial freedom sees a striking change in the nineteenth century. While the pastoral landscape sets free ambulatory subjects such as Aristotle and Wordsworth, the city has become more and more commanding as a new setting for walkers. The romantic tradition of walking in nature still exists; nevertheless, urbanization not only replaces the rural landscape with city streets as the dominant habitat of walkers but also complicates the relationship between strollers and their social space. The Baudelairean *flâneur*, strolling in the city without a specific destination or purpose, defines freedom as the right to derive pleasure from wandering in the streets and pretending to be what he isn't. For the leisure-class *flâneur*, walking as a means to explore the shifting social space is also a persistent attempt to assert his privilege of being at home in the world, one of the most extreme forms of the open space imaginable.

Technology and global capital redefine the act of walking: these two determinants dramatically change urban *flâneur's* habitat, his ways of walking, and the sights he sees with his footsteps. If walking is access to an open space, and globalization appears to blur the boundaries between human beings and their living environment, one has to ask the question: is walking in the global city an epitome of spatial freedom? According to Michel de Certeau, pedestrians' unplanned footsteps are transgressive and liberating in a world constructed by the panopticon power: the macro-discourse of the urban system cannot contain the wild footsteps of city walkers; rather, it is the pedestrians' performative act that (re)shapes the city. I would like to consider the possibility that the subversive power of walking in the global city may be more illusory than what de Certeau argues. Before we glorify the liberation of walking in global cities, we have to ask what pedestrians de Certeau has in mind: are the footsteps of low-paid workers as transgressive as those of white-collar managers? Also, how does globalization act upon the city-walkers? Given the fact that global culture is one within which physical boundaries can be repeatedly redrawn to promote all kinds of global flows, such as those of money, people, ideas, machinery, and images as Arjun Appadurai describes, the myth of an open space catering to pedestrians is necessarily transformed by the specific cultural-economic dynamics of the global city (33). This study will seek to contribute to the question of how the ideology of open space in global cities has been appropriated, rewritten, or complicated by agents of different social groups.

The historical trajectory of walking seems to show that the global city has become the ultimate habitat of walkers. In fact, the global city registers a historically unprecedented phenomenon in terms of the size and density of human population, the complexity of infrastructures and construction, and the mobility of capital, information, commodities and people. The question of how global cities change the everyday life of their urban inhabitants thereby requires rigorous analysis. Among the theorists of global cities, John Friedmann, Anthony D. King, and Saskia Sassen are of paramount significance in terms of shaping the "global city model." For Friedmann, world cities designate the nodal points of capital flows:

> ... the world economy is defined by a linked set of markets and production units, organized and controlled by transnational capital; world cities are the material manifestation of this control, occurring exclusively in core and semi-peripheral regions where they serve as banking and financial centres, administrative headquarters, centers of ideological control and so forth. (qtd. in King 12–13)

Drawing on Friedmann's conceptual framework of the world city, King affirms that "[t]he most inherent feature of the world city is its global-control function and this gives it its principal geopolitical characteristic" (25).

Friedmann's and King's definitions of the world city as a command-post site for global capital are further elaborated by Sassen, who defines the world city as "the global city" which "represents a strategic space where global processes materialize in national territories and global dynamics use national institutional arrangements" (1998a: 478). Specifically, global cities "function as international business and financial centers are sites for direct transactions with world markets that take place without government inspection" (1996: 216). Engaging in a full-scale analysis of the global city, Sassen contributes much to the research on the complex relationship between metropolises and the globalization of capital. Her studies bring to light that the widely recognized imaginary of geopolitical decentralization one encounters in a global city is actually underpinned by a network that she calls "a new geography of centrality and marginality" (1996: 210). This is a network that facilitates logistics with the advancement of technology to assure the fast return of profit or "time-space compression" in David Harvey's words. Based on her field studies, Sassen proposes to understand the global city as a dual city with the intensification of two classes — the new elite or the international business people and the low income "others."[4] The international business people's claims to the urban space produce the "glamour zone" of the city, embodied by the impressive skyscrapers, whereas the marginalized people's claims to the city are often naturalized as non-existent. Sassen's dual city model points to one way to the concealed spatiality, the uneven development of the global city that is often glossed over by government officials, urban planners, or multinational corporations as "our shared future," a prosperous space of hope for every inhabitant regardless of their gender, class, or ethnic identity.[5]

Henri Lefebvre, an insightful thinker who pioneered the investigation of the tangled relationship between the details of life and space against the background of globalization, also offers many suggestive theories for us to further explore the complicated relationship between urban everyday life and global cities. His *Production of Space* highlights the presence of the "lived space", largely ignored by the rational and epistemological theories of space, so as to illuminate the discrepancy between how the space is mapped out scientifically — the representation of space — and how it is experienced emotionally — the representational space.[6]

Reviewing contemporary literature on globalization and metropolises, I define the global city as the urban space that has been intensively subjected to the global flows of capital to the extent of compressing the living space of the inhabitants in the service of capital accumulation in the last two decades.[7] Capitalist space such as landmark office buildings, fancy hotels and restaurants, and international airports often expands at a galvanizing speed and takes over the prime areas of the global city. For example, Hong Kong's Chek Lap Kok International Airport and Hong Kong Disney transformed the quiet Lantau Island to a land of convenience for international business people and tourists. In Tokyo, the metropolitan government urges the citizens to "make room" for Tokyo to become a global financial and trade center. The large-scale urban rezoning in the business district and the skyrocketing rent in the urban center leave the middle and lower class Tokyoites not many choices but to move to the distant suburbs, with long commuting hours a routine nightmare of the day. Shanghai's urban development in the 1990s particularly demonstrates how global capital changes the landscape of the city. The cluster of dazzling skyscrapers in Pudong and the newly constructed buildings everywhere in the whole city account for the disappearance of the traditional alley houses and relocation, voluntary or not, a shared experience for the majority of Shanghainese.

Given the unprecedented speed and massive scale of the formation of the global city, the morphology of the Pacific Asia metropolises is more radically transformed to facilitate capital flows in the last two to three decades than that of Western global cities such as New York and London. While the urban spaces of London and New York were originally formed by forces of Industrial Revolution, nationalistic expansion, and local business growth before globalization, those of Asian global cities can be seen as the products of capital globalization, which gathered its full momentum in the 1980s. To be precise, the landscape of Hong Kong, Tokyo, and Shanghai has been shaped predominantly during the campaign of their "global city formation." The urban space and discourse of these three cities thus serve as pertinent examples to demonstrate the interconnections among city users, public space and capital globalization as seen in East Asia megalopolises.[8] Statistics show that between 1970 to 1990, Hong Kong's GDP rose fifteen-fold, and exports twenty-seven-fold: the city saw its most amazing economic growth in the mid-1980s (Yeung 17). Similarly, Tokyo emerges as a leading global city in the 1980s: the Japanese TNCs increased from 35 in 1975 to 90 in 1987, 84.6 percent of the 1,251 foreign companies had headquarters in the city, and the Tokyo Stock Exchange ranked the second largest in the world (Yeung 31). Shanghai, the uprising global city of the Pacific Asia was integrated into the world economy in the 1990s. In 1993 Shanghai mobilized more than 1 million construction workers for its key construction projects, and the next year 9,580 million US dollars' foreign direct investment flowed in. For Shanghai to discharge its function as a nodal point of global transaction, one-fifth of the world's construction cranes are in intensive service. The urban development we saw in Hong Kong, Tokyo, and Shanghai exemplifies the rise of Asian global cities as the best site to examine the effects of globalization on the urban space.

Inspired by Walter Benjamin, I venture to call the theoretical framework of my discussion of walking in Hong Kong, Tokyo and Shanghai a montage method. Benjamin's method of undertaking the archeology of modern life from individuals' walking and seeing in the city, attempting a "double exposure of past and present" to comprehend modern life through the knowledge of the past (Buck-Morss 1986: 109), opens a window to a micro, private approach to understand what Lefebvre defines as the representational space. Susan Buck-Morss rightly calls this a montage method (1986: 99). While Benjamin superimposes the past and the present, my project juxtaposes social and literary discourses. In each chapter I superimpose the social account of the city's urban space as reshaped by the process of globalization with the private account of registering the urban landscape experienced by its walkers, as represented in the films of Wong Kar-wai and Shinya Tsukamoto and the novels of Wang Anyi. With an interdisciplinary nature, the montage method that juxtaposes these two accounts, urban discourse and artistic work, manifests both the divergence and the intersections between the highly aggrandized official narrative of globalization and the private sensory experience of walking in the global city.⁹ The interaction thereby proposes a constellation that may contribute to grasping the gap between the representation of space and the representational space, the problems of living and walking in a city increasingly defined by global flows.¹⁰

Part One of this book will employ Hong Kong, a prominent East Asian global city, as an example to explore the walking of the *flâneur* in twentieth-century global cities and the ideology of open space. Buck-Morss argues insightfully that the *flâneur*, the renowned nineteenth-century city roamer, is actually "more visible in his afterlife [in the contemporary era] than in his flourishing" (1986: 105). As Rob Shields maintains, the importance of the figure of the *flâneur* lies in "its utopian presentation of a carefree (male) individual in the midst of the urban maelstrom" (qtd. in Tester 67). The cityscape of the nineteenth century seduces the *flâneur* with the illusion of infinite spatial freedom. We might ask if the era of globalization also presents the contemporary *flâneur* with such walking space to assume individual liberation from the traditionally defined social space (public/private, home/streets) and social relations (self/crowd). I would like to explain why the Baudelairean *flâneur* in the global city might not be able to enjoy being at home in the world. *Flâneurs* in Hong Kong have been subscribing to the image of their city produced by the official and the multinational consortia as a free land of opportunities. Is their knowledge of Hong Kong a reasonable speculation or an inflated myth?

To answer this question, I juxtapose the social/historical account of Hong Kong's urban development in response to globalization with Wong Kar-wai's 1994 film *Chungking Express*. I argue that Hong Kong as a global city is a space of dual compression. The global compression refers to the vast urban space restructured for Hong Kong to fulfill its role as a hub of transnational capital, for example, the construction of the new international airport and the landmark business buildings. The local compression means the consequences of the global spatialization such as the influx of foreign laborers and the severe housing problem for ordinary people who have to jostle for living space with the top-level professionals coming to the city with the global flows. Wong Kar-wai's *Chungking Express*, telling the story of four lonely walkers' frustrations and longings in the Hong Kong streets, provides a key to the problem of embracing Hong Kong as a convenient door to all kinds of possibilities while the monumental space that nurtures this global dream is more for the transnational corporate workers rather than for everyone that walks its sidewalks.

Part Two focuses on the changes in the urban space and people's everyday life brought about by the globalization of Tokyo with a particular emphasis on how the city-user might respond to the contradiction between living in an ever-compartmentalized and compressed space (what one experiences) and imagining to be part and parcel of the global city, a corridor to the world as the epitome of an open space (what one conceives the city to be). The juxtaposition of the official account of Tokyo as a preeminent global city famous for its technological progress and power of capital with the private account of contemporary Tokyo as a space where walkers are oppressed by the urban jungle of steel and concrete in Shinya Tsukamoto's horror films suggests the problematics embedded in the logic of producing the global city. As Anthony Giddens reminds us: globalization is "a process of uneven development that fragments as it coordinates," so is the global space a site of contradiction (qtd. in Yeung 9). Tsukamoto's films, the *Tetsuo* series and *Tokyo Fist,* show an extreme case when a docile salaryman, the ideal citizen of the global city Tokyo, is overwhelmed by the city of high-rises to such an extent that he mimics the space he inhabits and turns into a killing machine so as to blend in. The striking violence enacted by the films' protagonists can be read as a reaction to the global city formation, which not only renders much urban space to serve capital accumulation but also requires the inhabitants to identify with the drastically different city at the cost of losing more and more of their concrete space of everyday life. Mimicry, a term originally used to describe the living organism's imitation of their environment in order to survive the power of the space, thus becomes a dominant trope for us to recognize the violence of the global spatialization often imposed on the local people in the name of urban development with a pass to the open world on the table as the most seductive chip.

Part Three attempts to elucidate how Shanghai's rise as a global city in the 1990s brings to light the production of such a global space and its problems. After China's open policy in 1978, with its glamorous past as a cosmopolitan city in the 1920s and 1930s, Shanghai emerged on the map of the nation and the world as the most promising member of the global club. Exploring the urban discourse and the actual development of Shanghai's transformation into a global city, I argue that Shanghai is made in the image of existing global cities such as New York, London, Tokyo and Singapore.

The logic is that the built environment and the social structures of Shanghai have to be rebuilt before it can work as one of the centers of the global economy. We might say that Shanghai was not born as a global city as many claim with the city's cosmopolitan past as evidence, but becomes one because of the ambition to attract capital flows. The process of remaking Shanghai into a global city shows how the capitalist space takes precedence and subjugates the lived space of local people's everyday life. Moreover, the uneven development as seen in other global cities cannot be overlooked in Shanghai's case: the rise of the new elite class including expatriates and local "successful people" parallels the marginalized "blind flow" of migrant workers flowing in from neighboring provinces. While copying the image of a global city as a success story to pass on, the urban planners or government officials downplay the dual city problem as we saw in those "role-models."

Shanghai writer Wang Anyi's works, dedicated to the details of Old Shanghai life in the traditional housing, the alley houses (*lilongs* or *longtangs*), help us to see the gap between the dazzling new look of the city and the vanished Old Shanghai represented by the minutia of daily life in the *lilongs*. While the grand narrative of Shanghai regaining its old glory encourages the city-dwellers to envision being (re)connected with the world, the strong sense of loss and nostalgia experienced by the walkers in Wang Anyi's works narrate a different story of living in the global city. Wang's zealous efforts to supplement the glittering monumental space of the new Shanghai with the details of everyday as she remembers in the Old Shanghai reveals one critical oversight of making the city in the image of the global space at the expense of the lived space of daily life. Yet, more significantly, the writer's obsession with filling out the void, i.e., the ignored details of daily life, as she sees in the global Shanghai, endorses the official slogan of the global city formation: "Development is the irrefutable truth." Wang envisions globalized Shanghai as what she has to work on with an insider's memories and experiences rather than a cultural and economic construct as a result of globalization. Obsessed with the "lack" of contemporary Shanghai, Wang leaves unanswered how it becomes a global metropolis and the social problems entailed by the globalization.

Time-space compression (space and time collapse to facilitate flexible accumulation) has given rise to accessible catch-phrases such as "the global village" and "this is a small world."[11] Yet for many of the inhabitants of the global city, the "shrinking world" phenomenon is deeply literal: the lived space of everday life is shrinking to make room for rezoning, construction of infrastructures, space modification — all in the name of urban development. The contradiction between the widely disseminated belief in an open space that enables us to be connected with the world and the fact that the here-and-now lived space is subjugated to the capitalist space might not be an unhappy coincidence of modern life. The fact that global capital penetrates every corner in the world does not equal to maximum spatial freedom for every user of the global city. Moreover, physical boundaries can be transgressed but not erased. Before embracing the global city as a space of freedom for those who walk its streets and sidewalks, first of all we will have to clarify whose open space is enabled by the social infrastructures of global cities. For money to flow without obstruction at the fastest speed imaginable, capitalism has been producing such urban spaces that can be defined with terms like "decentralization, openness, possibility of expansion, no hierarchy, no center, no conditions for authoritarian or monopoly control" (Sassen 1998b: 177). Yet the open space embodied by the global city for the capital accumulation is paradoxically confining and oppressive for many of the city-users.

PART ONE

Hong Kong Blue:
Where Have All the *Flâneurs* Gone? Walking in Between Eternal Dual Compression

> With cities, it is as with dreams: everything imaginable can be dreamed, but even the most unexpected dream is a rebus that conceals a desire or, its reverse, a fear. Cities, like dreams, are made of desires and fears, even if the thread of their discourse is secret, their rules are absurd, their perspectives deceitful, and everything conceals something else.
>
> Italo Calvino
>
> To me it [*Chungking Express*] feels like a diary or a map. All the scenes were shot according to the logic of the place. If you go to Hong Kong after seeing *Chungking Express*, you won't get lost.
>
> Wong Kar-wai

In Part One of this book I intend to superimpose the social/historical account of Hong Kong's urban space as subjected to a dual compression between the local and the global with the representation of Hong Kong's cityscape experienced by its walkers in Wong Kar-wai's film *Chungking Express*. In so doing, I hope to provide a study of Hong Kong, generated through the dialogue between these two versions of the same city, to articulate questions with regard to the new myth of globalization lingering in contemporary Hong Kong. Chapter One, an illustrative rather than exhaustive interpretation of Hong Kong's urban space, brings to light to what extent and in what ways Hong Kong's urban space has been shaped by the forces of a dual compression. Global compression refers to space collapsing to serve the purpose of global capital accumulation, and local compression, space collapsing to accommodate urban densities of population and housing, aggravated by global compression. I will give concrete examples to illustrate not only the spatial changes engendered by global compression, such as, among others, Hong Kong Disney and Chek Lap Kok International Airport, but also the changes engendered by local compression in response to globalization and its demands, for example, overpopulation and public housing. The urban discourses will be followed by Chapter Two, a critical reading of Hong Kong director Wong Kar-wai's 1994 film *Chungking Express*, with a particular emphasis on the director-as-*flâneur*'s impressionistic mode of representing the city and a detailed analysis of the walkers marooned in the dream evoked by the global city mirage. The concluding section focuses on the interaction between the above two stories of Hong Kong, seeking understanding of the global city from the montage of the official account and private account, the disjunction and conjunction between the narrative and images of the film, and the rhetoric and rationale of the urban development blueprint.

1

Hong Kong:
A Nodal Point of Dual Compression From British Empire Colony to Disney Kingdom Outpost[1]

November 1999: 28 months after the 1997 handover of sovereignty from Britain to China, Hong Kong has once again attracted the spotlight on the international stage, this time with its decision to join the kingdom of Disney. A correspondent report in *New York Times*' travel section unfolds the story of Disney's joint venture with socialist China, an enterprise unthinkable before the age of globalization.

Hong Kong's tourism commissioner, Mike Rowse, sees this as a golden opportunity to revitalize the declining number of tourists since 1997. A common anxiety over the fading splendor of the "Pearl of the Orient" is translated into a high hope of becoming one of the few Disney family members in the world: "[w]e kind of faded out of the spotlight after 1997, and everybody wrote us off.... This project [Hong Kong Disney] tells the world that we are alive and kicking." Mike Rowse voices the official account of the urgent need to get the crowd back. Predictably, the hotel business also looks forward to the Disney project. "It will be a boon for all the hotels, because it will put Hong Kong back on the map," says a former director of Shangri-La hotels.

What is Disney's story? Why is Hong Kong their choice of a new home for Mickey Mouse in Asia, after Tokyo Disneyland? The report notes that Disney executives are fascinated by Hong Kong's cosmopolitan disposition: "Hong Kong's international character was a key reason they chose it over Shanghai and other mainland cities that were lobbying to be the site of the first Chinese Disneyland." Judson C. Green, the chairman of Disney's theme-park division endorses Hong Kong as "always an incredibly exciting city" regardless of the regional financial crisis. While his definition of "exciting" remains unspecified, Green's tone is as excited as that of Mike Rowse. Another reason for Hong Kong to stand out among Asian cities lies in its built environment: "Mr. Green said Disney was also attracted by Hong Kong's infrastructure. With a spectacular year-old airport and a gleaming network of roads, railways, tunnels and bridges, Hong Kong is one of Asia's easiest cities to get to and get around in."

A common response on the part of readers to the news of Hong Kong Disney is, "where are they going to put it?" — it takes some magic to find such a space in overcrowded Hong Kong for Disney's magic kingdom. Hong Kong authorities solved this problem by making the best use of "a quiet bay on Lantau Island," the big island west of Hong Kong, conveniently situated between central Hong Kong and the new airport.[2] Lantau Island, one of the few places in Hong Kong that remains less commercialized and globalized, will undergo a radical change from an underdeveloped nature resort to a clone of Disney's fantasy land. How do people in Hong Kong react to this millennium project? Are they as eager as the tourism officials or the Disney executives? The *New York Times*' report ends with a comment on the local reception, which seems to be so typically Hong Kong: "Hong Kong seems willing to bear the cultural baggage of Disney so long as it brings the crowds back. Besides, *people here are used to foreign powers with global ambitions*" (emphasis mine). Notably, in the *New York Times*' report of the changing spatial forms, the global narrative, underwritten by Disney Company, somehow coincides with the local needs, seemingly shared by the tourism authority and local people with global dreams. In the following discussion, I would like to closely examine the validity of such a coincidence.

Disneyfication of the City: The Global Compression

This impending global project of a Disney theme park on Lantau Island, expected to open in 2005 and to be fully completed in 2020, exemplifies the dominant driving force behind Hong Kong's urban space, the power of globalization, which penetrates the local space for its own purpose of facilitating capital flows. Hong Kong Disney, as the conclusion of the report suggests, speaks for the "foreign powers with global ambitions," a concrete example of international mobile capital and its concomitant effect of time-space compression. Like other command-post cities in the world, Hong Kong is a nexus of global flows, which compress space and time to facilitate the agglomeration of capital. David Harvey defines such time-space compression as a phenomenon "generated out of the pressures of capital accumulation with its perpetual search to annihilate space through time and reduce turnover time" (1990: 306–7). Time-space compression gives rise to a shrinking world (space compression) and simultaneity (time compression) (Bridge 612).

New technologies in communication and transportation speed up turnover time in both production and consumption; the accelerating turnover time in capital further demands the disappearance of spatial barriers.[3] The intensity of time-space compression in the global age thus points to an era of simulacra as such: ". . . it is now possible to experience the world's geography vicariously, as a simulacrum. The interweaving of simulacra in daily life brings together different worlds (of commodities) in the same space and time" (Harvey 1990: 300). "Harvey's Lefebvrian scheme implies that the material context of experienced, lived space is defined by the spatial imaginings of those with more power in capitalism" (Bridge 614).[4] Global compression is a process of eliminating our sense of history and creating a homogenized space through technologies, a make-believe "small world" in Disney's magic kingdom, where physical or temporal boundaries have to be traversed to serve the purpose of assuring a fast return of profit: a depthless space as Fredric Jameson describes.[5]

Such globalization not only brings about specific spatial forms but also entails a new social structure in the city. Saskia Sassen sums up the new urban geography of global cities as one in which unbridgeable differences arise between two types of city users, a small proportion of international business people (the new elite) and a huge population of low-income "others" (the underprivileged) (1996: 221). Of particular interest in my discussion of global compression is her observation on how the urban landscape is determined by the new user of the city.[6] Sassen contends that for the international business people, the ideal city is one "whose space consists of airports, top level business districts, top of the line hotels and restaurants, a sort of urban glamour zone" (1996: 220). The claim of these "humble servants" of the global capital empire is rarely challenged or questioned; the urban infrastructure thereby is transformed as the new actor's sphere of action in the city becomes increasingly influential.

The story of Hong Kong Disney evidences such claims of city space by foreign powers — new city users, here Disney executives, prize only the spatial forms that contribute to the internationalization of capital — hotels, an airport, and a network of inland transportation. The infrastructure of Hong Kong has been built and rebuilt to fit into the utopia of transnational business, a city subscribing to economic liberalism with all necessary facilities, and such long-term accumulation of claims from its new users makes Hong Kong the chosen home of Disneyland.[7]

Nothing serves as a better illustration of the profound influences of global compression on Hong Kong's urban vistas than the city's monumental space, the "glamorous zone" as Sassen portrays it. By monumental space, I refer to what Lefebvre means by monumentality, anchors or converging points of a "large social space covered by networks or webs" (222), represented in Hong Kong's urban structure by skyscrapers. Monumentality signifies "the will to power," the desire to command time (subdue death) "through the intervention of the architect as demiurge" (221). Such a spatial form, according to Lefebvre,

> always embodies and imposes a clearly intelligible message. It says what it wishes to say — yet it hides a good deal more: being political, military, and ultimately fascist in character, monumental buildings mask the will to power and the arbitrariness of power beneath signs and surfaces which claim to express collective will and collective thought. (143)

Monumentality in Hong Kong's urban contexture is best manifested by its distinctive capitalist architecture, i.e., the skyscrapers that assume the functions, forms, and structures of monuments. Global compression requires monumental buildings not only to serve as command posts but as Lefebvre points out, as a mirage of collective will, in Hong Kong's case, a will to achieve phenomenal economic success from its liberal economic system and global city status. Concentrated in Central, "the Wall Street" of Hong Kong, the cluster of impressive high-rise buildings thereby becomes a poster shot of Hong Kong, a stamp of Hong Kong's global cityness.

The monumental space in Hong Kong expands from the upscale Central to its adjacent area, an area where global compression renders old communities obsolete. The case in point here is the re-development of decrepit Old Wanchai neighborhood from Suzie Wong's home[8] to a satellite area for Central, manifested by the presence of more and more high-rise buildings. With a long history of expansion, these examples of "placeless" architecture as Ackbar Abbas calls them — predominantly multinational corporate buildings, hotels, international banks, and shopping malls — continuously move eastward toward the adjoining harbor side area Wanchai, a famous "recreational" bar area particularly popular with soldiers and sailors in the 1960s.[9] Due to the fact that large corporations compete with each other for prime space in the city, building and rebuilding becomes inevitable outcome of such a will to power. With the growing need of global flows and the increasing cost of land and space in Central, the golden space for multinational corporations, more and more space in Wanchai thus is monumentalized, sandwiched by Central and Causeway Bay, two of the most highly developed commercial zones in Hong Kong. It seems unavoidable for Wanchai to be "rejuvenated" by the urban plan of connecting Central, Wanchai, and Causeway Bay. International buildings (office buildings, shopping centers, restaurants, and hotels) now occupy the reclaimed land north of Gloucester Road in Wanchai: "With new business coming in from Central, it may be a matter of time before much of the Wanchai that many visitors have known and loved comes under the demolition jackhammer" (62).[10] Kevin Rafferty's lament over Wanchai's expanding monumental space registers the invading power of global capital and its indelible imprints on the urban landscape.

Hongkong and Shanghai Banking Corporation (HSBC) Headquarters and the Bank of China Tower, two of the most distinctive capitalist monumental buildings in Central, also enable us to perceive how the dynamics between global compression and monumental space inscribe the urban geography.[11] Built by the British architect Norman Foster, HSBC Headquarters, a 52-story steel and glass skyscraper, reputed to be "the world's first billion-US-dollar building," was constructed with the ambition of erecting the tallest bank in the world for 50 years to come (Rafferty 56).[12] The Bank of China soon proves such expectation a pompous joke. Looking down the city across the road between Garden Road and Cotton Tree Drive, the Bank of China Tower, a 72-story skyscraper made of glass, steel, and marble, was built by Chinese American architect I. M. Pei. It soon became the new landmark of Central (after 1989's opening) physically for its height, and metaphorically for the changing dynamic of political dominance. For China, claiming the tallest monumental building in Hong Kong endows the Beijing government a panoramic view, which renders the city legible and controllable. The Bank of China also functions as a silent but most salient reminder of China's sovereignty to Hong Kong residents, to the previous colonial government, and to the international forces. Most importantly, this bamboo-like skyscraper anticipated socialist China's increasingly active role in the global economy. The Bank of China, the dazzling door of the Beijing government in the south, opens to global capital flows converging in Hong Kong.

These two competing banks elucidate Lefebvre's definition of buildings as "the homogeneous matrix of capitalistic space" (227). Put in Freudian terms, Lefebvre conceives the power-infused buildings as "'condens[ing]'

The Bank of China Tower and other high-rises.
(Picture taken by Mary G. Padua in 1996)

relations of abstract power, property and commodity exchange into particular sites... [and] 'displac[ing]' activities into socially controlled and specially equipped sites" (Pile 212). In other words, such skyscrapers compress space and time according to the various requirements of capital. As Abbas rightly observes, regardless of the architects' strenuous efforts to physically differentiate the Bank of China Tower from HSBC Headquarters, "the spatial logic of these two buildings belongs to the same international architectural system. . . . What the city's built forms themselves tell us is the very different story of 'one system' (that of international capital) at different stages of development" (1997: 85). Noticeably, the monumental space reveals the ideology of global capital compression, which then exposes the political ideology of China's "one country, two systems" prescription for the Hong Kong Special Administrative Region (SAR). The "food chain" suggests the complicit structure of global flows and nation-state — through monumental buildings they fabricate a collective dream for the city-users.

A tour to Lan Kwai Fong in Central presents another case of the global compression mechanism in Hong Kong. A highly gentrified area full of stylish bars and restaurants with names of exotic places, Lan Kwai Fong is a miniature Disney World, in which time and space become commodified. Situated on the periphery of Central, Lan Kwai Fong started in the early decades of the twentieth century as a quiet residential area. In the seventies, it becomes the home of quite a few artists due to its comparatively cheap rent and its location in Central (Leung 90). Dressed up by its image of "Soho," Lan Kwai Fong, an "anonymous urban vernacular," appeals to entrepreneurs as a potential commercial space (Abbas 1997: 87). With the trend of globalization since the 1980s, Lan Kwai Fong has been converted into an area of fancy cafes, bars, and discos. Specifically, Lan Kwai Fong exemplifies how the new city-users' (international business people) claims determine the urban landscape as such: the landscape of Lan Kwai Fong becomes a phantasmagoric international enclave, the "Montmartre" of Asia, with restaurants and bars emerging like weeds on its European cobblestone streets. The names of these "hip" meeting places signify a strong sense of cosmopolitanism: "California," "Central Park," "American Pie," "Casa Blanca," "Beirut," "Indochina," "Thai Silk." Certain names defy our sense of time: "The '50s," "Club 64" (referring to June Fourth 1989, the Tiananmen Square massacre), "Post 97," and "Mecca 97" (Leung 91). For all the astounding variety, the kaleidoscopic names on the surface indicate a space that is anywhere but here, and "a sense of time that is always not the present" (Leung 91). Concealed beneath the image of Lan Kwai Fong is the mechanism of time-space compression: the space that indicates elsewhere is a simulation, a compressed shrinking world, while the time that refers to either the past or the future actually signifies temporal compression, a simultaneity in which there is nothing but the present.

The Hong Kong poet P.K. Leung's essay "The Sorrows of Lan Kwai Fong" reveals the emotional response to the inscription of global compression in the city. For Leung, Lan Kwai Fong epitomizes Hong Kong's hybrid culture: "East and west; past, present, and future; they are all crammed here, freely, haphazardly." It creates an image of "an open space where all kinds of people can gather — expatriate and local; people from different walks of life" (91). However, such an image is nothing but a formulaic repetition of the "melting pot" ideology. After the 1992 New Year's Eve accident, which caused 20 people to be trampled to death by the crowd in Lan Kwai Fong, the Hong Kong government attempted to regulate this area, most outrageously censoring a professional photography exhibit and auction (Leung 92–3).[13] The anecdote Leung gives helps us rethink the myth of "open space:" the mixed space invites users to invest emotionally or financially, seducing them to claim the space for their own purposes, but the political and economic forces working behind the "open space" seldom reveal themselves to the users.[14] The story of "Happy Together" at Lan Kwai Fong is a sentimental rationale for global compression, which registers a source of sorrows for those who long for something more than a theme park of global space:

> Lan Kwai Fong always makes me think of Hong Kong. The space we have is a mixed, hybrid space, a crowded and dangerous space, carnival-like even in times of crisis, heavenly and not far from disasters, easily accessible and also easily appropriated — by political, economic and other forces.... This space that is open to us can all too easily be lost to us. (95)

Leung narrates the sorrows of Lan Kwai Fong, a lost space for many Hong Kong people, an inverted form of Benjamin's enchanting phantasmagoria whose source always remains hidden.

The last example of global compression in Hong Kong is the airport, a quintessential urban built form that serves as an index to the intensity and influence of globalization in the city. The new airport project at Chek Lap Kok, Lantau Island, demonstrates the effects of globalization on urban plans and the city's infrastructure.[15] It is notable that from the very beginning the new airport project appeared to be a political concern more than an economic one. Hong Kong's old airport, Kai Tak, has for a long time been regarded as inadequate for the growing demand, but it was not until after the Tiananmen Square massacre that the colonial British government put forward the new airport project as a sign of confidence in Hong Kong's future under the sovereignty of communist China. The seemingly altruistic motive behind this proposed construction of a US$21 billion international airport is seen from China's viewpoint as a scheme to drain Hong Kong's financial reserves. In response to Governor Chris Patten's remarks that the new airport should be seen as a "dowry" bequeathed by the departing British father instead of as the financial burden described by the Chinese government, Premier Li Peng is reported to have replied: "During the more than one hundred years of its role, which began in 1884 [sic], the British Empire took away much more wealth than the 'dowry' it will leave in 1997" (Yahuda 72–3).[16]

There seems to be no disagreement over the location of the airport, despite the fact that the huge cost of the airport can be partly attributed to the chosen construction site at the northern shore of Lantau Island, which requires the construction of not only the airport but also the necessary infrastructure, including highways, bridges, and a transit system to transport passengers and freight between the island and Hong Kong or Kowloon. Lantau Island, a less developed place on the map of Hong Kong's urban planners, has fewer than 30,000 inhabitants, compared to a million on Hong Kong Island (Rafferty 92). Obviously, it is neither China's nor Britain's concern if Lantau Island's residents do not welcome the grand project as a gateway to the future, the profit that makes up for the shattered peace, as the government officials try to convince them. Disney's project, proposed less than two years after the new airport opened for use, proves the function of the new airport as a symbol of the hope of keeping Hong Kong as one of the world's top command-post cities. The changing spatial configuration on Lantau Island is to open for a more diversified use of global capital. This vernacular space, once used as a retreat for various religions, now faces a future with Mickey Mouse and Donald Duck as their prestigious neighbors against a background of the scream of jet planes.

Often politicized to be a wager in the tug of war between China and Britain before the 1997 handover, Britain and China's dispute over the huge budget of the new airport project unwittingly conceals the importance of another player in the project, i.e., international capital.[17] Notably, neither party denies the justification of constructing a new airport to replace Kai Tak Airport, whose limited capacity as the only international airport has been agreed upon by all concerned with the increasing demand of globalization in Hong Kong. Regardless of its objection to the cost, China anticipates the new airport to register post-97 Hong Kong as the international transportation hub in the South China region, and, more importantly, as a global city with massive international connections, which will facilitate China's growing ambition in the global economy before any inland city takes over.[18] By the same token, closely examined, Britain's rhetoric of justifying this mammoth new airport project — such as Sir Percy Cradock's remarks on the plan as "efforts on our side to restore confidence in Hong Kong" — reveals Britain's ambition to maintain Hong Kong's capacity for concentrating global capital, despite the shift of sovereignty in 1997, a shift which posted a potential financial risk for investors (Buckley 132). Specifically, the crux of such a grandiose rationale lies in the question of whose confidence Britain endeavors to restore. On the surface, Britain attempts to present this case as "a very determined exercise to boost public morale," the colonial father's effort to keep his Hong Kong children from leaving (Buckley 132). Yet this large infrastructure project is actually more a last attempt to prevent global capital from leaving, or, to be more precise, to accumulate more global capital by involving huge foreign loans in the construction.[19] Indeed, Chek Lap Kok Airport was constructed predominantly as a monumental space for international investors, in the name of encouraging Hong Kong people by assuring the continuity of their global dream, overshadowed by the June Fourth Incident.

Not Just the Tourists: Local Compression and Public Housing in Hong Kong

The open space rhetoric that P. K. Leung employs to describe Lan Kwai Fong finds a magnified version across Victoria Harbor in Tsim Sha Tsui, at the tip of the Kowloon peninsula, a district calibrated to the tastes of foreign tourists. Tightly packed with hotels, restaurants, nightclubs, and shopping centers, Tsim Sha Tsui has been famous not only for its glittering "Vanity Fair" extravaganza but its crowded, hybrid urban spectacle. If Central represents the utopia of global capitalists, Manuel Castells's informational city with the accumulation of capital flows opaque to the local inhabitants, Tsim Sha Tsui stands for the visible temples of Mammon, with the incredible pedestrian flow as the embodiment of a gold mine for both global and local investors. At issue here is how a city of slightly over 400 square miles accommodates such a large number of walkers on the streets. What do we know about Hong Kong's urban space through the density of the housing? Transparently, not all of the walkers brushing shoulders with each other on Nathan Road are tourists with shopping bags staying at fancy hotels.[20] I intend to use Tsim Sha Tsui's overcrowded urban spectacle, another all-time favorite poster image of Hong Kong, as a little Hong Kong cameo to examine the spatial changes under the compression of global flows, i.e., the local compression.

To highlight how global compression (re)inscribes Hong Kong's cityscape, my discussion seeks to explore the causal relationship between the concentration of urban population and Hong Kong residents' congested living space. Hong Kong's overpopulation is an inevitable consequence of the city's long history of involuntary immigration and globalization, despite its continuous emigration since the 1980s. With an average outflow of 50,000 to 60,000 people per annum, Hong Kong still witnessed a rapid growth in total population in the 1990s (Skeldon 1995: 303). For one thing, Hong Kong's geographic position and political status attract Vietnamese boat people: in 1989 more than 20,000 Vietnamese boat people "had fled and taken shelter in the colony" (Rafferty 484).[21] Hong Kong has also been a refuge for mainland Chinese people since World War II. By 1951 the total population of Hong Kong reached 2.5 million due to the large numbers of refugees crossing the

Chungking Mansion on Nathan Road, Tsim Sha Tsui.
(Picture taken by the author in September 2002)

border from China, a 0.8 million increase in a decade (Rafferty 148). Two other massive flows of Chinese immigrants took place from 1960 to 1963 and from 1978 to 1981 (Wong 90). From 1993 onward, with the 1997 handover approaching, the daily quota of new immigrants from China increased from 75 to 105. Globalization during the last two decades brought in not only international business people but also imported laborers, a congregation of low-paid workers. As a regional center of Southeast Asia and Southern China, the global capital accumulated in Hong Kong draws in laborers from less developed countries in the area, for example, the 80,000 Filipino maids in the city.[22] The emergent infrastructures to facilitate global capital flows such as the new airport project, further demand construction workers from outside of its own labor pool, in this case, the Chinese laborers from neighboring Guandong Province.[23] The huge number of imported laborers reflects the new international division of labor — a dichotomized concentration brought about by the trend of globalization: the accumulation of capital generates many low-income jobs as well as high-paid managerial and professional jobs, with glaring disparities between their wages. In addition to legal migrant workers and immigrants, for years there have been numerous illegal immigrants crossing the border to Hong Kong, predominantly for economic reasons.[24] The numbers of illegal immigrants caught and repatriated increased from 10,000 to 12,000 per annum between 1981 and 1984 to 43,000 to 44,000 in 1992 and 1993 (Skeldon 1996: 190).

Consequently, the influx of immigrants, imported laborers, and refugees jostle for space in a city whose land is monopolized by the state. For years housing has been the most pressing concern in Hong Kong, as a result of overpopulation.[25] No evidence accounts for the interrelationship between global compression and local concentration better than Hong Kong's public housing. I would argue that the high-density anonymous housing projects, an antonym of the monumental buildings such as the Bank of China Tower or HSBC Headquarters, are spatial/architectural expressions of Hong Kong as a dual city under the impact of globalization. In essence, the cramped living conditions in the pigeonhole high-rise residential buildings articulate local hyper-densities, against the backdrop of an arresting global capitalist showcase, exemplifying how global influx, in complicity with the state's own interests, decidedly circumscribes the relatively fixed and limited local space.

The issue of public housing in Hong Kong can never be dissociated from the meaning of land and space and the state's policy of land development. Tightly packed high-rises, highly subsidized by the government, have been the only housing offered to almost half of Hong Kong's population.[26] Yet this apparent rational solution to utilize the limited space of Hong Kong for its over 6 million inhabitants is an ideology imposed on the public to enforce the British government's priority of land use in the colony. The official account of the housing project never fails to foreground the scarcity of land and the overpopulation problem due to the continuous flows of immigrants, two undeniable facts of Hong Kong's urban geography. Nevertheless, residents have not been made aware of certain facts, such as that the government's Housing Authority is one of the world's biggest landlords, or that the government's arbitrary zoning of "rural" and "urban" ensures all kinds of restrictions on using the "rural" land, thus confirming the scarcity of land and its soaring price (Abbas 1997: 86).[27] All of the land and space in Hong Kong is basically the state's commodity, on auction to the highest bidders, a game for the state as well as other rich players, such as multinational consortia or local entrepreneurs.[28] The intention of massive public buildings presents less a concern for the available living space for local people than a strategy of reclaiming more land for the state to manipulate. Examining the issue from a historical perspective, we witness a functional, profit-seeking motivation behind the public housing projects. These urban developments started as the government's response to the 1953 Christmas fire at the Shek Kip Mei squatters, which left 50,000 people homeless. But the resettlement of the squatters is for economic reasons rather than reasons of social welfare:

> . . . they [squatters] are resettled because the community can no longer afford to carry the fire risk, health risk and threat to public order and public prestige which the squatter areas present, and *because the community needs the land on which they are an illegal occupation. And the land is needed urgently.* (Lai 191; emphasis mine)

Under the façade of an amazing philanthropy project unfolds a story of high-handed land development control. As Alan Smart argues, from the beginning housing projects have been closely related to the state's own interests "in attempting to preserve its extensive control over the development process and its long-term revenues potential from its monopoly over land ownership . . . " (48). Public housing, in the official account of history, a solution to the homeless squatter-inhabitants after the big fire, soon turns out to be a mechanism to clear other squatters for more land to develop.

Two examples help us recognize how the space of local ordinary citizens is compressed by the requirements of the global economy as well as how land use in Hong Kong has always been contingent on economic profits defined by the state. In the mid-1980s, the government adhered to a development control over urban densities through the "planned conversion of mixed commercial/residential uses into totally commercial uses (notably of offices and hotels)" (Lai 201). Offices and hotels, spatial forms gratifying the new users of the global city, designated the land-use hierarchy in Hong Kong. The demands of capitalist accumulation, galvanized by globalization since the 1980s, are the number one priorities in the blueprint of the state's minimalist town planning.[29] Likewise, since the mid-1980s four Regional Development Strategy studies, Metroplan, addressing the issue of the future supply of land for public housing, reiterated the same logic of prioritizing capitalist needs in terms of land use. The official solution to urban density lies in saving the land and space for office buildings or hotels in the hope of gradually transforming the Metro area to a pure commercial zone:

> [T]he Metro Area would not have net growth in population or housing units notwithstanding massive reclamation and hill terracing. The objects are to thin out population and allow for expansion of the office and hotel sectors....

> The Metro Area would remain as the major territorial employment centre
> especially for office work. (Lai 204)

As a result, public housing had to be dispersed to less developed rural areas such as Lantau Island and the New Territories, where urbanization has steadily eradicated most of the signs of agricultural life and unsettled the old communities.[30]

Competing with the state-owned land and the space of transnational corporations for industrial or commercial purpose, the lived space of ordinary Hong Kong people is congested to such an extent that the average space of a public housing inhabitant ranges from 2 square meters per person to 5.5 square meters per person (Cuthbert 1987: 144).[31] Regardless of the incredibly unsatisfying nature of this quotidian living space, the demand for such jam-packed public housing is on the rise.[32] Given the escalating price of private housing rising to HK$6,000 per square foot for small and medium size apartments by 1994, local people are left with no better choice (Lai 188). To meet the demand of public housing, the Housing Authority decided to put up new blocks on sites in housing estates currently used as open space or car parks (Lai 189). Since the land that could have been used for housing has been used for commercial or industrial purposes, or been saved by the state to serve such purposes in the future, the Housing Authority may well claim that their hands are tied. Therefore, it is justifiable to make room for housing by taking over the public space. Whose public space is it anyway? As Alexander Cuthbert suggests,

> the urban forms of collective consumption [public housing] had the highest economic priority and the lowest economic input. They were relegated to the cheapest available land with the highest density of development. They materialised in highly compressed, modular forms at the level of the dwelling, the storey, the building unit, the spatial sub-division, and the total layout. (1987: 144)

The Hong Kong government's chronic desire to reserve the free operation of its urban space so as to be ready to make room for profitable spatial forms contours Hong Kong's urban environment as a nodal point of compression: the monumental space of global capital congested with grand office buildings and hotels is made possible through compressing the living space of ordinary people. The high-rise skyscrapers with corporate names in Central in a sense are built not with glass and metal but with the space taken from the anonymous high-rise buildings whose majority inhabitants have no easy access to the global monumental space or the information flow. The conflicting functions of these two types of high-rise buildings thus signify the segregated social space, a reality that might de-mystify the narrative of the global city as a space open to all of its users. Seen in this light, Hong Kong illustrates Sassen's dual city vistas — the transnational corporations' monumental skyscrapers surrounded by jam-packed public housing point to an ever-widening gap between the dazzling representational space for the global flows and the hyper-dense representation of space for the local people.

2

Chungking Express:
Walking With a Map of Desire in the Mirage of the Global City

Wong Kar-wai's *Chungking Express*, a 1994 urban film about the sensory experience of walking in Hong Kong, vividly illustrates how walking as a spatial practice interacts with the global city, where global and local compression come into play. In *Chungking Express*, walking is a compulsory activity for the city-dwellers: a personal attempt to create more space, physical or imaginary, commercial or social, ephemeral or enduring, under dual compression of global flows and local concentration. Specifically, the film delineates the walking experience in a conflicting space that oscillates wildly between yearning and frustration, resulting in an unbridgeable gap between the micro perception and the macro account of the global space. In the discussion below, a brief summary of how walkers in the film savor bitterness and sweetness in turn offers a close reading of the main characters' respective walking journeys. My exploration aims to examine how the *flâneur*'s habitat in the metropolis, redefined by technology and global capital, changes the experience of walking and seeing in the city.

Space of Fantasy/Map of Desire

Chungking Express contains two stories about four walkers, two policemen and two women: among the labyrinthine storefronts, beehive buildings, dingy

---

This chapter is developed from the author's article of the same title in *Quarterly Review of Film and Video*, 18, no. 2 (2001).

apartments, crowded streets, these walkers respectively map out their own paths of desire, their desire to cope with the disconnection they feel from the city, to probe the living space of others, and to dream their global dreams. Their highly compartmentalized and interiorized living space, circumscribed by the dual compression in Hong Kong, aggravates the emblematic sense of isolation and loneliness rampant in a big city. Walking, as a daily practice, crystallizes the walkers' longing for more space, a longing particularly poignant in Hong Kong, one of the most populated cities in the world. In a sense, walking becomes therapeutic for the alienated walkers: it serves as an antidote, to temporarily relieve the syndromes resulting from "wondering lonely in the crowd," the unbearable malady of being left out in a big city. Walking makes what lies beyond the limited private space seem accessible.

In addition, the widespread hyper-dense beehive buildings in Hong Kong intensify a characteristic yearning of city walkers, deepening their voyeuristic curiosity about the invisible space of others. The walkers in *Chungking Express* display such desire to expose the hidden corners of the architectures/buildings of the city maze, de-compartmentalizing the mysterious beehive space, and mapping out a legible city for themselves. Most significantly, the flow of global capital continuously holds out promises of globalization for local people, an inevitable trend with its trademark space as one of freedom, convenience, chance, and fluidity. Living and walking in such a space, people in Hong Kong are spoon-fed the glorious global dream, which assures a most prosperous space for all of its city-dwellers. The fast changing spatial configuration in Hong Kong emerges as a consequence of this long-lasting global dream, which takes the form of daily reality. The urban space of Hong Kong embedded within such a narrative of global progress thus turns out to be a space of fantasy for its walkers to inscribe their own desires and dreams, a space glossed over by the grand rhetoric of globalization.

Lost in a Big City: Global Space as a Mirage

The four walkers in *Chungking Express* are connected in some way at sometime in the city, but the chance encounters seldom entail reciprocity. Reciprocity implies a return gaze that haunts the *flâneurs* since Baudelaire's time. Their yearning for intimacy appears to be doomed, and despite their knowledge of Hong Kong, these walkers are disoriented in the city. Why do their journeys in the city convey a strong sense of loss and melancholy? I suggest we start with the walkers' cognitive mapping of their city space: what do they know about global space?[1] How do they experience the global city as they brush shoulders with millions of others on daily basis? Is the "global space" the walkers encounter in everyday life the monumental space in Central (studded by skyscrapers like the Bank of China Tower), the tourist district in Tsim Sha Tsui (home of fancy hotels such as the Peninsula), or the rich residential area in the Peak? If not, what corners on the map of Hong Kong correspond to the "lived" global space for these walkers? I would argue that the deeply ingrained belief in their global city as a space of convenience and opportunity for everyone proposes a way to grasp the walkers' frustration from walking in the global city. The glamorous zone of Hong Kong is promulgated by the official account of the global city to such an extent that it becomes the only visible space. Consequently, these walkers cannot see the dubious nature of the inflated global city: a convenient door that invites them to fantasize all kinds of possibilities camouflages an invisible wall indifferent to their desires and dreams.

Femme Fatale or Disoriented Dupe? The Woman Walker With a Blonde Wig and a Wrong Map

The first walker's desire and frustration, centering on an incident of transnational heroin smuggling, serves as a textbook example of being fatally anesthetized by the ideology of global city as a place where dreams come true, dealers and dreamers alike. The opening shots of some run-down buildings introduce us to this mysterious woman walker: an Asian with a blonde wig, sunglasses, and a raincoat.[2] The image of this *femme-fatale* walker plays on the stereotype of female "streetwalker," a prostitute who goes after her business in the street, an enigmatic beautiful sexual object whose walking in the city attracts the male gaze in film noir.[3] Yet the business of *Chungking Express'* *femme fatale* is not prostitution but drug dealing, and the attempt to eroticize her walking meets with discontent.

First this unknown woman walks to connect her supplier and the hired hands; she then walks in the city all day with a gun looking for her Indian accomplices after they disappear at the airport.[4] What this *femme fatale* expects from walking in the city is personal material gains from transnational capital flows. It is a long standing myth that Hong Kong offers nothing if not the opportunity to make money, a commercial space for all, and our mysterious woman walker is not exempt from such an ideology.[5] From a trendy bar to hidden corners of the beehive building, from mean streets to the airport, she walks in the city with an inflated map provided by the official account of Hong Kong as a global city, a materially well-endowed metropolis where one can always find the means to better-off days. The blonde walker's over-investment in the smooth capital transactions via Hong Kong, legal or not, makes her an ill-fated dupe in the game from the very beginning.

The female drug-smuggler's walking highlights three sites that demonstrate different aspects of the dual global/local compression in Hong Kong: a bar in Central, Chungking Mansion in Tsim Sha Tsui, and the Kai Tak Airport, each deviating from her imaginary global city respectively.[6] The path she takes to reach her global dream turns out to be a nightmare, because of her optimistic reading of these global spaces as convenient, controllable, and legible. Before visiting the dark corners of Chungking Mansion, the woman walker stops by the bar where her "boss" and lover, a white bartender, gives her a paper bag presumably filled with heroin and money. Little does she know that he actually betrays her and sets her up. A closer look at the locale helps to explain her apparent gullibility. What deceives the *femme fatale* is more the environment of the drug deal than her unfaithful partner: a fashionable bar with a white bartender at downtown area epitomizes global space to her. Her map says Hong Kong is a city where global flows converge and in her experience the bar appears to be the perfect nodal point of the global flows. The locale of the bar as a symbol of global dreams therefore makes the transnational deal look like the "real thing" to her.

The inflated map of Hong Kong's urban space takes the walker to her next stop, the famous Chungking Mansion of Tsim Sha Tsui, a tourist area famous for five star hotels and fancy shopping centers. Following her footsteps, we enter into the hidden corners of the Chungking Mansion, a rundown beehive building with numerous suites and multi-ethnic inhabitants. The building exemplifies one characteristic space generated by the local and global compression: hybrid, congested, and pigeonholed. Its interior in fact conjures up an impression of a street full of unknown pedestrians, most of them dark-skinned, suggesting the ethnic identities of the residents. Mingling with strangers on the narrow hallways in this dark, crowded building, the blonde-wigged woman steps into the suite of the Indians, who are supposed to transport the drugs for her. A sequence of quick shots shows the audience details of the deal such as the exchange of passports and US currency, the professional help from local tailors and shoe makers in the same building, and the tricks of hiding the drugs in every possible place in the "tourists'" luggage and body. These shots actually echo the woman walker's gaze:

everything seems to be under her control. An abject suite in Chungking Mansion, a hidden corner of the global space, facilitates the money flows just as efficiently as any other part of the whole city machine. Not until she loses these Indians at the airport, one of the essential urban infrastructures that represent the global compression of space, is the woman agonizingly aware of the missing links in her calculated plan.

Dealing with the mixed space in Chungking Mansion with a map that maximizes the global dream and minimizes everything else, including potential threats, the blonde-wigged walker is bound to lose control of these Indians. In her misleading map the seedy hybrid space of Chungking Mansion signifies a contemporary version of the nineteenth-century slum, a resentful pollution in the "clean and proper" city of the bourgeoisie.[7] Yet the nameless woman's profound belief in Hong Kong as a space of convenience turns the rundown slum to a reservoir of cheap labor at her mercy. Obviously, she visits the squalid corners of the global city with an out-dated mental version generated from nineteenth-century European cities, identifying these Indians with a stereotype of slum-dwellers, abject and thus docile enough to carry out her criminal scheme. In other words, the inhabitants of the shabby corners of Chungking Mansion are nothing but inferior sub-humans. Her condescending arrogance toward her accomplices-to-be is revealed as soon as she steps into the suite: the shot of her sitting in front of the refrigerator trying to get some cool air implies her being out of place.

In a manner that recalls an inverted form of an urban planner of a concept city, who finds capital sufficient to de-slum the abject space, the blonde walker believes money alone can manipulate these foreigners, who flood into Hong Kong in search of opportunities to make money. Presuming an "appropriate" abject space for these "foreign laborers," she denies the possibility that they can be agents of intelligence and culture. This partly explains why she cannot imagine that the hired Indians will outwit her and abscond with the drugs. All of these details point apparently to the woman's impaired mapping ability, following from her preconception of the city — under the spell of global and local compression — as one in which all kinds of dealings are possible and money walks in every corner of the city, be it decent or dirty. In her mind's eye, the "slums" are just another backdoor open to cheap labor, which exists for no other reason if not money flows. Her wearing sunglasses all the time suggests her blindness to the changes taking place in a global city. Likewise, her behaving as one out of place in the corner of the Indians' room hints at her inability to map out the space of her partners. As a result, it seems natural for her to lose sight of them in the clean and proper global space — the international airport — where the fake decent tourists disappear under her nose near the airline counter. Her frustrated deal marks a false mapping of the global city, an unavoidable outcome of not being able to see what is there.

Considered closely, the mysterious woman's seemingly spontaneous appeal to a stereotypical imagination of the slums can be seen as an expedient reaction prescribed and circumscribed by globalization. As a city walker who has no easy access to the information flows circulating in the international banks or multinational consortia, i.e. the legal dealings of global capital transaction, she is confined to a fragmentary understanding of her environment by an unreliable map. Always situating the woman in dark and obscure corners of the city, the film implies her inability to transcend the spatial limitations to reach for a full picture. The mysterious woman is doomed to mistake her limited vision, broken perspective and facile understanding of the global space for objective and rational spatial mapping. In other words, she takes her vision of the global space to be reality; the inflated map is regarded as an authentic one.

Throughout her journey, disorienting sequences of fragmentary camera images significantly echo the debilitated gaze of the female walker. The audience is denied the chance to see a complete picture of the suite or the building where the drug smuggling takes place. The interior of the building is presented as a combination of broken pieces: shots of different corners resembling pieces of a jigsaw puzzle — an eatery, a foreign cash exchange counter, an elevator, labyrinthine hallways, a shabby toilet, and small double-deck beds. The fragmentary urban images as well as the woman's impaired gaze contrast with the invisible map she resorts to, a map produced from a panopticon view with monumental space as the poster landmark of global flows, a seed bed of global dreams for those who walk on Hong Kong's sidewalks and streets.

After her frustrated attempt to recover her lost drugs, the mysterious female walker loiters in a bar. Her disappointment is analogous to the frustrated sexual relation experienced by the two male *flâneurs* in the film. Noticeably, both *flâneurs* are police officers, the reminder of state apparatuses: Cop 223 in the first story is an undercover officer, Cop 633 in the second story a low-rank patrol officer. Their profession as agents of law and order seems to be the only residual motivation for them to map out stable social relationships. These two police officers end up being nothing more than incompetent *flâneurs*, either blind to the obvious or unable to interpret what they see.

From police officers to *flâneurs*, the shift of their roles in a sense suggests the declining importance of state apparatuses in global cities.[8]

Multilingual as Global: The Talking *Flâneur* Looking for a Return Gaze

The first *flâneur* we encounter, the undercover cop 223, displays a classical yearning for intimacy in a metropolis from the very beginning of the story: "we rub shoulders with each other everyday. You may not know each other. But we could become good friends someday." With such expectations in mind, *flâneur* 223 walks and talks to be reconnected with others, to find a return gaze, to establish a relationship that refuses to "expire" too soon. Walking is his attempt to create a social space in a promiscuous metropolis where proximity and reciprocity do not go hand in hand. His measurement of the distance between himself and the blonde-wigged woman he passes by reveals not only his romantic longing for reciprocity but the dramatic differences the tiniest space makes to people walking in a space of dual compression: "At the closest point, we are only 0.01 cm apart from each other. In 57 hours, I fall in love with this woman." Like many other city-dwellers, 223 walks to cope with the acute loneliness of living in a compressing space.

This cop-turned-*flâneur* defines his global city as a multi-lingual, hybrid space composed of various ethnic communities. Walking and talking in the city, 223 imagines being connected with others instead of just passing by the anonymous crowd and thus repeating the sexual frustration experienced by Baudelairean *flâneurs*, the melancholy of "love at last sight."[9] *Flâneur* 223's first attempt to create some social space by speaking multiple languages takes place in front of the fast food counter, Midnight Express, where he makes phone calls from the public phone in the hope of reaching for substantial interaction after being jilted by his girlfriend, May. The shot of the setting suggests the global space 223 experiences on a daily basis: the fast food joint serves as a microcosm of Hong Kong's compressed space. A "next door uncle" type of guy runs Midnight Express with local workers and foreign laborers changing at the speed of people walking through a revolving door. This small shop front located at the periphery of the glamorous Central district shines with a colorful Coca-Cola neon sign, echoing those high-rise office buildings in the same area dazzling with multinational corporate names. Midnight Express is nothing fancy, selling multicultural fast food from chef's salad to Middle Eastern barbecue. Yet the owner's habit of chatting with his customers attracts the lonely *flâneurs*; Midnight Express thus turns out to be a stopover for both cops in the film. This multicultural global space represented by Midnight Express is a miniature of the global city as experienced by 223, physically adjacent to the tall buildings in the same district but functionally apart from the captivating skyscrapers.

In front of the multicultural fast food counter, 223's telephone marathon starts with May's parents, seeking a vicarious intimacy with his ex-girlfriend but in vain. They keep the conversation curt with polite distance. 223 then tries his luck by making three calls to female acquaintances from the past. He speaks to these women in Cantonese, Japanese, and Mandarin Chinese over the phone, hoping that speaking their languages can overcome the distance imposed by time and space. None of these women satisfies 223's longing for a return gaze. The shot of the dangling receiver of the public phone parallels the lonely walker in the street, suggesting his fruitless search for an imaginary community.

Like the archetypal *flâneur* Benjamin portrays, 223 is deprived of the experience of the aura, the emotional association with the world:

> [L]ooking at someone carries the implicit expectation that our look will be returned by the object of our gaze. Where this expectation is met . . . there is an experience of the aura to the fullest extent . . . . Experience of the aura thus rests on the transposition of a response common in human relationships to the relationship between the inanimate or natural object and man. The person we look at, or who feels he is being looked at, looks at us in turn. To perceive the aura of an object we look at means to invest it with the ability to look at us in return. (1969: 188)

The expectation of the reciprocal gaze is an index to the *flâneur*'s desire to communicate with others, to establish a substantial interpersonal relationship. However, instead of returning his look, the crowd moves on with "inhuman makeup." To be more specific, the *flâneur* in a modern city is doomed to experience melancholy in the crowd since what he is looking for, an intimate local community, is gone forever from the city. Confronting a heterogeneous metropolis made up of different kinds of communities, 223 still clings to his belief in a homogeneous social space. Multilingual proficiency is thus imagined as his magic power of retrieving the lost community: he not only looks but talks while walking. Ironically, he cannot see what is there, and all he hears is finally the echo of his own mumbling.

Flâneur 223's frustration from imagining the heterogeneous global space as one that can be broken down into different homogeneous communities through languages is best demonstrated by his chance encounter with the blonde woman in a bar, where he approaches this mysterious woman in four languages. After her futile hunt for the runaway couriers, the woman drinks alone to vent her anger and frustration from walking all day in the city. Subject to the stereotype of a single woman drinking alone, 223 attempts to chat with this "broken-hearted" woman in different tongues. Unable to pin down her identity right away, 223 has to ask the same question four times — in Cantonese, Japanese, English, and finally in Mandarin Chinese. Patronizing the seemingly fragile woman, 223 chauvinistically offers generous consolation, saying in an understanding tone that it is so obvious to him that a woman can only wear sunglasses at a bar for three reasons: she is blind, pretentious, or heart-broken. Beyond doubt, a pretty woman like her falls into the last category. His multilingual vocabulary fails the occasion; ironically, here the hunter/prey signifier instead of pointing to the police/criminal oppositional pair (an undercover officer is supposed to find out this woman's illegal dealings), turns to signify the melodramatic sexual relation between man and woman. As a plain clothes cop, 223's understanding of global space is boiled down to a promiscuous multicultural society, with language proficiency his only pass to the segregated compartments.

Circumscribed by his global dream, the *flâneur*/officer is fated to miss his prey. The two of them end up in a hotel room, with the exhausted woman walker sleeping in bed, and the *flâneur* eating chef's salad and watching Cantonese dramas on TV. The *flâneur*'s desire to eroticize his potential prey in a private space, usually associated with women, remains unsatisfied on account of his narrow definition of the global city. He might be able to speak her language, but it is naïve to assume that common languages guarantee reciprocity. The frustrated sexual relation between the *flâneur*/cop and the mysterious woman proves again the attenuation of the state's power and the always-deferred sexual satisfaction of the *flânuer*.[10] 223's chance encounter with the woman walker, first appearing as a love at the last sight on the street, indicates that 223 not only fails in his official job as a detective, but as a *flâneur*, traditionally shrewd and observant. Indeed, 223's habitual dependence on talking as the means to a return gaze reveals how the convergence of multiple languages and discourses in a global city, easily translated to the ideology of a melting-pot community, becomes another version of the global mirage spellbinding its pedestrians.[11] Conflating the totality of social reality in the global city with multilingual, a single linguistic phenomenon of a multicultural society formed by the interaction of global and local compression, the *flâneur* derails himself from his quest for an accessible social space.

For *flâneur* 223, talking serves as a shock defense in a global metropolis where he is unable to retrieve his loss of an intimate local community, crystallized by his ill fortune in love.[12] The impossibility of returning to an imaginary past, in 223's situation a fervent yearning for romantic love, fosters the emotion of nostalgia. Facing the double compression of Hong Kong's urban space, a *flâneur* like 223 experiences accelerating shifts of desire and frustration without an end. Hong Kong is a city of more than 6 million people, a city of chance and coincidence. What are the odds of not being able to find true love if one walks and talks as much as possible? Rey Chow's account of the nostalgia experienced by Hong Kong residents helps us comprehend 223's frustrated quest for eternal love in a space at the mercy of a dual compression:

> In the 1980s and 1990s, the omnipresence of real estate speculation means not only that "original" historic places are being demolished regularly, but also that the new constructions that replace them often do not stand long enough—to acquire the feeling of permanence that in turn gives way to nostalgia—before they too are demolished. (1998: 135)

Globalization and its manipulative compression inflict a sugarcoated affliction, whose source remains unrecognizable. Unable to find the return gaze, 223's failed attempts to retrieve the lost community with his multilingual proficiency herald the mire of melancholy, which takes the form of nostalgia.[13]

The pineapple episode spells out the nostalgia of a *flâneur* looking for compassion in a city of compression. Breaking up with his girlfriend May on the first of April, he decides to wait for her one month, which is evidently an excuse for him to disavow the fact that May will never come back to him. During this period everyday he buys one pineapple can that expires on the first of May, as pineapple is his girlfriend's favorite fruit. Displacing his desire to hold on to his lost love/space into the act of buying pineapple cans, 223 seeks to recover the sense of order and stability.

223's conversation with the salesperson at OK convenience store expresses a strong sense of the *flâneur's* nostalgia.[14] Upon addressing the question if they still carry pineapple cans that expire in two hours, the clerk tells 223 to get something fresh; nobody wants expired goods. 223's ensuing accusation marks out the archetypal nostalgia, a longing for harmonious relationships between subject and object in a world less dominated by technology, consumption and rationality than his Hong Kong: "People like you always go for something fresh. You know how much effort is put in a can of pineapples? The farming, the cropping, and the slicing. Throwing it out like that. Have you ever thought about the can's feeling?" Obviously, 223 identifies with the thrown away pineapple cans: the fast changing global space disrupts the auratic relationship between self and other. His quixotic ideal is unthinkable for the clerk, who voices a much more pragmatic and cynical viewpoint: "Buddy, I sell here. And I have to think about the can's feeling? Have you thought about my feelings? The loading, more loading, and unloading. How I wish those cans won't expire. That'd have saved me lots of work!" Life is too short to be philosophical. Frustrated by their conversation, 223 steps outside of the store to sit on the stairs, pondering, "[s]omewhere, somehow everything comes with an expiration date. Swordfish will expire. Meat sauce will expire. Even Glad wrap will expire. I wonder if there's anything in the world that won't expire?" Through the camera's eye, we see 223's lonely figure, a dark shadow with only silhouette visible. Notably, this dark figure contrasts with the background of the convenience store, a colorful world of commodities which has forgotten the process of production: the wine shelf basked in the bright lights, the fridge filled up with foods and drinks in the store, and the gigantic ice cream advertisement dazzling below the glass window of the storefront. The nostalgic *flâneur* is an anthropological species facing the danger of extinction in the world where turnover time predominates. The scene that seems to foreshadow the demise of nostalgic *flâneurs* in a global city is disrupted by another passing shadow, a small old lady who picks up whatever she can find of value on the streets, an updated form of the nineteenth century rag picker. 223 figures she might appreciate the value of expired cans and thus share with him the mourning for what cannot be found in the city of commodity. Again his search for a return gaze only invites blunt rejection: "Expired cans? I don't want them."

223's resistance to the expiration date along with his plan of buying pineapple cans for a month to defer the loss of love signifies a shock defense in the form of creating an alternative, private temporality to counter the devastating time-space compression imposed by global capital flows. When 223 is ultimately fed up with those piles of cans, he realizes that what he incorporates is the canned pineapple rather than his lost love. His idiosyncratic means of healing his broken heart can be interpreted as a vestige of the nineteenth century *flâneur*'s attempt to put off the loss, analogous to the Baudelairean *flâneur*-poet's efforts of elaborating the "love at last sight," which registers more than anything else the melancholy of walking in a modern city.[15]

Airport/Global Space/Women: The Self-pity *Flâneur*

While *flâneur* 223's global dream is cacophonous, *flâneur* 633's is monotonous: the only audible sound in his global dream, the roar of airplanes, has been magically transcribed to a serenade of love. 633's obsession with flight attendants and airplanes implies that for this cop-turned-*flâneur*, airport embodies the global spaces, a synonym of sexual relationship in his lexicon. The spatial form which caters to the demands of the new user of the city, the white-collared service class in the global city ironically becomes the quintessential global space for someone outside of this class, a low-rank patrol officer, who spends most of his time walking in the streets rather than flying in and out of Hong Kong. Throughout 633's journey, his fascination with airplanes and flying parallels his yearning for love. Against the backdrop of an airplane taking off, 633's voiceover narrates his brief relationship with a curvy flight attendant: "On board every flight, there must be an attendant you want to seduce. This time last year 25,000 feet above sea level, I successfully seduced one." Next shot introduces us to his apartment with 633 flying a model plane in his hand, chasing his flight attendant girlfriend in her bra and uniform skirt. After sex he plays with the miniature plane over her naked body, the voiceover telling us where the rest of the story goes: "I thought we two would stay together a long time, flying all the way like a plane with a full tank. I didn't know the plane was going to change course." Jilted by his girlfriend, 633 thus became lost in the global city. He copes with his loss by going home and confiding in the inanimate objects such as his towel and soap, instead of reaching out for others like his colleague 223 does.

In fact, being short-leashed by the chain of global dream and women for so long, 633 no longer looks forward to any exciting chance encounters with the crowd: the urban space where he promenades everyday becomes invisible to him once the woman, a figure of the only global space known to him, high above in the sky beyond his reach, disappears from his daily life. Deprived of his global dream, domestic space turns to be the last shelter for this frustrated *flâneur* in the city. A shot that juxtaposes an airplane flying in the broad blue sky with his ex-girlfriend's uniform blouse on a hanger flying in the wind on the roof of his apartment building vividly illustrates 633's vanished global dream. This image, one of the few exceptional shots of open space throughout the whole film, is a follow-up of his talking to the blouse in his room: "Why are you hiding? I've been looking for you. One must face the reality. Don't hide. You are dirty. It looks like you are in the wrong season. Let's go sunbathing tomorrow." The juxtaposition of the ex-love's blouse and an airplane flying in the sky in one shot can be seen as a montage that reveals 633's yearning for a romantic relationship and his global dream as two sides of the same coin.

The devastated *flâneur*, losing receptiveness and interest due to the disappearance of the only recognizable global space in his everyday life, is later redeemed by the re-connected link between the two essential signifiers, women and global space. 633 compares his expectation of a new relationship to cleaning up the runway at the airport for the arrival of another flight. At the "California" restaurant in Central, 633 waits for Faye, the Midnight Express girl who has a huge crush on him. Again he resorts to the rhetoric of flying to describe his still up-in-the-air romantic relationship: "I arrived at California earlier, as I suspect there's going to be a delay." A shot of blurred crowds passing by in the background highlights his loneliness. After a while, he mumbles to himself that he has a hunch the flight has been cancelled. Faye leaves him an envelope with a hand-written boarding pass valid in a year, a rain check for their romantic relationship. The truth is that she comes to their date much earlier before flying to California in the USA that night. Finding out that the flight changes course unexpectedly, 633 talks to a beer bottle in the restaurant, convincing himself that Faye does come to California, just another one: "she was there that night, just a different place. The two of us went to California that night. Only there was a time difference of 15 hours. The time now at California is 11 AM. At 8 PM will she remember she has a date with me?" The two Californias, California in the US, and the trendy restaurant named California at Lan Kwai Fong, come into play with 633's global dream. All the fancy bars and restaurants with the names of foreign places at Lan Kwai Fong create the illusion that Hong Kong is a microcosm of the world and that the global space is within easy reach. However, that night at the California restaurant *flâneur* 633 painfully grasps the physical distance between the two Californias.

Interestingly, no more confined by the narrow space of Midnight Express, Faye "flies away" when 633 finally gets ready to start a relationship with her. When she comes back as a flight attendant, dressed the same as his ex-girlfriend, the link between woman and global space seems to be completely restored. Their story finishes with a dramatic role change at Midnight Express: 633 as the owner of Midnight Express standing behind the counter talking to Faye, the flight attendant, at the other side of the counter. Showing her the blurred "boarding pass" as a token of promise and affection, 633 starts to indulge in his next cycle of global dream.[16]

California Dreaming in Hong Kong: The Female *Flâneur* as a Mirror

While the blonde-wigged woman and the two cops-turned-*flâneurs* in *Chungking Express* point to the gap between the private and public accounts of Hong Kong as a global city of dual compression, the last walker, Faye, a female *flâneur*, elucidates the global effects on strolling in the city, crystallizing police officer 633's *flâneurie* as an allegory of walking in contemporary Hong Kong. Faye's improvised walk, from Midnight Express through local street markets to the apartment of officer 633, fleshes out not only an image of the female *flâneur* in a global city, but also the rampant effects of global mirage on the walkers, embodied by officer 633's numbness to the fast changing environment in the global city. Such numbness as a negative reaction to the global metropolis is an extreme form of what Georg Simmel explains in "Metropolis and Mental Life," "the blasé attitude" urbanites develop toward the overwhelming stimulus of city life:

> [t]here is perhaps no psychic phenomenon which has been so unconditionally reserved to the metropolis as has the blasé attitude. The blasé attitude results first from the rapidly changing and closely compressed contrasting stimulations of the nerves. . . . A life in boundless pursuit of pleasure makes one blasé because it agitates the nerves to their strongest reactivity for such a long time that they finally cease to react at all. (413–14)

The numbness is different from what Benjamin defines as "shock defense" in that the latter implies an endeavor to assert the consciousness of the self/subjectivity.

Faye is introduced to us as a lower-middle class girl, working for her cousin at Midnight Express. Originally she walks as a classical type of woman walker, whose justification for walking on the streets is shopping. Getting the key to 633's apartment from the envelope left by his flight attendant girlfriend, Faye transforms her journey of running errands to an excursion of desire. She extends her daily routine of shopping at traditional markets or paying the electricity bill for Midnight Express to 633's apartment. Her voiceover confesses her stray: "Yesterday I dreamed about visiting his place. When I left his home, I thought I would wake up. But for some dreams you will never wake up."[17] Instead of following the route prescribed for her, Faye sneaks into 633's apartment, justifying her detour by "sleepwalking." Refusing the rudimentary form of the female *flâneur*, i.e., aim-oriented walking, which precludes woman walkers from experiencing the city with an active gaze,

Faye magically turns her functional walking to an exciting stroll which displays the possibility of female scopophilia and an unhampered female *flâneur* on the streets of Hong Kong.[18] More importantly, her privatizing the officer's private space, the destination of her walk, traces the concealed link between the forces of globalization and its effects on the local walkers.

Faye's excursion to the hidden corner of the apartment of 633 exemplifies the voyeuristic desire of those confined by the compartmentalized space in the global city. For one thing, her active female gaze contrasts with *flâneur* 633's impaired vision. Seeing this apartment as her personal playground, Faye derives pleasure not only from cleaning up his house, but also from arranging various details of his private space in the hope of fashioning a new identity for 633. Yet 633 turns a blind eye to the differences, unaware of the fact that home has become a strange place transformed in every little corner. The new table cloth and bed sheets are as invisible as the tranquilizer put in the bottle of drinking water. He neither notices the increasing number of gold fish in the tank nor the changed photos on the mirror. The unobservant 633 does not suspect that someone deletes his phone messages and uses a magnifying glass to look for any clue to his sex life in his bed. His numbness to the changes in his private space is further elaborated by his quick acceptance of the changes around him. He talks to the Garfield stuffed toy, the replacement for his stuffed white dog, as if they were the same: "[w]hy do you turn yourself yellow? And a scar? Did you fight with anyone?" Eating his black bean sardine can, 633 puzzles at the striking similarity between tomato tuna (says the label) and black bean sardine (tastes the content), completely unaware that labels of the original sardine cans have been changed. The CD of "California Dreamin'," placed in his disk player by Faye, soon turns out to be his ex-girlfriend's favorite. When Faye asks him when he started to like this song, his answer is "I don't care. My girlfriend likes it." Here the common association between home and familiarity presents itself to be an irony. Frustrated by the global mirage while walking in the city, 633 turns to his private space as the last sanctuary of self-pity and consolation. Ironically, even his home is metamorphosed into a strange place without his knowledge. Indeed, *flâneur* 633 can be seen as an antithetical form of classical *flâneur* who enjoys the privilege of being at home in the world. It seems that *flâneur* 633 is homeless not only on the streets but also within his four walls.

633's slow response to the changes under his own roof is not beyond comprehension if we read it against Hong Kong's distinctive global space. Specifically, Faye's changing every detail at 633's apartment with her gaze corresponds to one significant consequence of global forces, that of defamiliarizing the familiar. To some extent, 633's blindness to the numerous changes in his private space is symptomatic of walkers in Hong Kong, who are constantly susceptible to the always changing urban space brought about by global and local compression. The speed of spatial change, a consequence of the disjuncture of dual compression, renders Hong Kong what Abbas calls a "space of disappearance." He points out that "[t]he combination of rising land prices, property speculation, and the presence of large corporations vying for prime space results in a constant rebuilding that makes the city subtly unrecognizable" (1997: 63). In other words, the social and spatial reality produced by the dual compression often outruns the walkers' perception and understanding. One common response to the overwhelming mutability of the global space is numbness, the waning affective in Jameson's postmodern terminology. Numbness registers a negative response to the changing lived space, where the sense of the order of things challenges recognition: "[t]he skewing of affectivity is the only 'content' and displaced index of such a space. It is a space that is at once very much there (in the effects it can produce) and not there (as directly discernible cause)" (Abbas 1997: 53). Seen in this light, 633 represents the "every man" walking in Hong Kong, suffering from what Abbas defines as "reverse hallucination," unable to see the obvious. Trained by the fast-changing sights in the global city, the inhabitants' gaze becomes less and less receptive to what is new and unique or what is obsolete and commonplace.

Faye's adventure at 633's apartment interestingly challenges the definition of private space as closed and secret: 633's yearning for global space, rendering his supposedly closed private space open and accessible to others, mirrors Hong Kong's status as a port city, opening up its space for global flows. What stands for global flows in the apartment episode is his ex-girlfriend, the beautiful flight attendant rather than Faye, then a local girl working at fast food counter. Faye can turn 633's home into a hotel room and herself into the voyeuristic maid because 633 has already opened up his private space for his girlfriend to come and go and arrange everything as she wishes. The flight attendant girlfriend, or in Faye's case, whoever gets the key, has as much right as 633 himself to his apartment. These two women's free pass to 633's private space allegorizes Hong Kong's local responses to global forces in two aspects. For one thing, the easy accessibility of 633's apartment suggests the consequence of the local, non-economic profitable space being invaded by the global flux, with 633 standing for the local, nation-state residue, and aggressive women, shifting manipulative global space. Furthermore, the local police officer's desire for the global flows, epitomized by his flight attendant girlfriend, embodies Hong Kong people's infatuation with globalization, an ideology formulated by the public account of the global city.[19] To the walkers on the city streets, spatial changes underpinned by such an ideology, shoved in their face everyday, are paradoxically overriding but indiscernible.

3
Between Representations of Space and Representational Spaces:
Flâneurie With the Camera's Eye

To lay out the interaction between the representation of space and the representational space in Hong Kong for a critical reading of the utopian discourse of globalization, it is essential to examine the director's gaze which mediates the walkers' experience of urban space in the film. I argue that Wong's *Chungking Express* is a *flâneurie*, or more precisely, a cognitive mapping of the director. Wong's attempt to offer an alternative but authentic map of his city through the routes and footsteps of his imploding *flâneur* identity, the multiple walkers in the film, confounds and at the same time confirms the overriding global space in Hong Kong.

Shock Defense and the Director-*Flâneur*'s Authentic Map of Hong Kong

Mapping Hong Kong with the camera and assuming the identity of the walkers on the street, Wong takes on the characteristic of a Baudelairean *flâneur*: approaching the reality of the vast terrain of city spaces with his interested and investigative gaze. In fact, the film *Chungking Express* can be seen as the director-*flâneur*'s shock defense, an attempt to make connections where experience is flattened out. Wong's project of mapping out the city with a private eye so as to reinscribe an authentic image of Hong Kong before it is

---

This chapter is developed from the author's article "Hong Kong Blue: *Flâneurie* With the Camera's Eye in a Phantasmagoric Global City" in *Journal of Narrative Theory*, 30, no. 3 (2000).

lost forever is an effort not too different from Benjamin's arcade project or the Baudelairean *flâneur*'s poem of retaining the moment of encountering his "love at last sight."[1] *Chungking Express* thereby materializes a *flâneur*'s mapping of the city: "[m]any people ask me if *Chungking* [*Express*] is a love letter I wrote to Hong Kong. But I'm not that romantic. *To me it feels like a diary or a map. All the scenes were shot according to the logic of the place. If you go to Hong Kong after seeing Chungking Express, you won't get lost*" (emphasis mine).[2] The apparent guide book rationale implies the director's ambition to capture the "logic of the place" in a city where spatial changes often outpace the revisions of maps due to its constant dual compression.

A beehive building: Chungking Mansion.
(Picture taken by the author in September 2002)

The urban spectacle the director-*flâneur* strolls through resists attempts to replicate or repeat the clichéd images of Hong Kong: Wong's intention is to present an insider's version, defamiliarizing Hong Kong before presenting an "authentic" interpretive grid of the city. The title of the film, indicating the two major sites of the film, Chungking Mansion in Tsim Sha Tsui and Midnight Express in Central, foregrounds the *flâneur*'s alternative take of the cityscape. Wong justifies such a choice in his interviews:

> It [Chungking Mansion] is a very famous building in HK [Hong Kong]. Statistics show that about 5000 tourists visit it every day. With its 200 lodgings, it is a mix of different cultures. Even for the people of neighborhood, it is a legendary place where the relations between the people are very complicated. It has always fascinated and intrigued me. It is also a permanent hotspot for the cops in HK because of the illegal traffic that take [sic] place there. That mass-populated and hyperactive place is a great metaphor for the Town herself.[3]

Along with Chungking Mansion, Midnight Express, the site of the second part of the film, located in Central's Lan Kwai Fong district, where "a lot of bars, a lot of foreign executives would hang out there after work," functions "as microcosms of Hong Kong."[4] Hence instead of showing the audience a well-promoted image of Hong Kong's glittering skyline, an architectural sign designating the city as "the Paris of the East," from the opening shots onward, the director-*flâneur* presents a Hong Kong unknown to the world. Against the evening sky stand some anonymous buildings with vertical pipes: the numerous protruding iron windows and the flying clothes on hangers suggesting a pigeon-hole life style of the inhabitants. Far from echoing the dazzling shot of Hong Kong's urban landscape at night, with the smog-like clouds swirling in the gray sky, these shots of the city's decrepit buildings succeed in sustaining a sense of unreal, or even quasi-*Blade Runner* sci-fi ambience of the city. Establishing the opening shots of an abject Hong Kong, the director-*flâneur* prepares the audience to explore the hidden corners of the city with the movement of his camera. The opening shots therefore suggest the director-*flâneur*'s choice in the first part of the film of the slum-like Chungking Mansion in Tsim Sha Tsui over any decent building with elegant shopping arcades or any world-famous hotels in the district. By the same token, in the second part of the film, a cheap fast-food counter in Central is the center of the *flâneur*'s gaze, rather than the monumental buildings or the trendy bars in the same area. For the director-*flâneur*, it is Chungking Mansion and Midnight Express instead of Bank of China Tower or Peninsula Hotel that constitute the "reality" of Hong Kong's urban spectacle as shared and dreamed by the local community.

Shock Defense and *Flâneur*'s Resistance to Modernization

If the quintessential Baudelairean *flâneur* signifies a force of resistance against the pace of modernization, *Chungking Express* as a chronicle of the director's mapping of the city signifies a similar shock defense of a *flâneur* engulfed in the signs and stimuli of the global flows.⁵ The film first re-incarnates the *flâneuresque* spirit in its leading characters. Given the congested urban space contoured by the global/local compression, Hong Kong in the global era hardly qualifies as a city for the *flâneur*, who "demanded elbow room and was unwilling to forego the life of a gentleman of leisure" (Benjamin 1973: 54). Walking in hyper-dense Hong Kong, insisting on elbow room is no less a fantasy than riding an empty subway train in rush hour Tokyo. Following Benjamin's definition, the walker in Hong Kong's streets is "the pedestrian who wedged himself into the crowd" (54). Similarly, most people in Hong Kong in their fast-paced urban life would find it difficult to relate to the classical *flâneur*'s habit of contemplating what he sees through strolling. Yet *Chungking Express* presents a convincing possibility of promenading in a global city. The two *flâneur*-turned cops might be unobservant and frustrated, yet the sense of leisure and a brooding interior landscape in the hustle-bustle of the city are far from unthinkable.

As the plot unfolds, the monologue of the plainclothes cop 223, imparting both his yearning for intimacy in the anonymous crowd and his protest against the expiration date on everything, hints at the director-*flâneur*'s defiance against the increasingly commercialized urban space, a seemingly inevitable phenomenon in the context of globalization. More importantly, the production of the film itself is a hallmark of the director's resistance to Hong Kong's commercialized cultural space. As an art house film director in the age of globalization, Wong is one of the few film makers who swim against the mainstream in Hong Kong's film market.⁶ An urban film that has no nude bodies or casinos, the two major selling points of numerous Hong Kong films after the 1980s, *Chungking Express* seeks to win the return gaze of the viewers with an elusive narrative and fragmentary images of an alienated Hong Kong. In parallel with the *flâneurs* in his film, the director is another stroller who moves through the crowd in the city with a sense of leisure that defies the speed of the flows of globalization.

Wong's mapping of Hong Kong through his camera's eye to some extent echoes Susan Buck-Morss's exposition of "author-as-producer:" "[t]he flaneur in capitalist society is a fictional type; in fact, he is a type who writes fiction. *Flâneurie* promoted a style of social observation which permeated 19th-century writing . . . " (1986: 111). What is of interest here is to what degree and in what aspects the *flâneur*-author-producer's account of social observation illuminates the lived space of Hong Kong in relation to the trend of globalization. For example, if we read *Chungking Express* against the official account of Hong Kong's urban space, how do we comprehend the gap or the repetition between these two versions of Hong Kong? I have already mentioned the role Hong Kong's cityscape plays in the film. However, we need to recognize that Wong's *flâneurie* somehow fails to represent Hong Kong as a polarized global city, represented by skyscrapers and public housing, the spatial configurations that reflect the urban development of the global era.[7] To be exact, Hong Kong as an entity cannot be reduced to the director's portrayal of Cheungking Mansion and Midnight Express. In *Chungking Express*, the *flâneur*'s gaze dodges the skyscrapers and the housing projects. The glamorous zone of the new city users — high-paid white collar occupations and activities — is absent, and the marginal class (residents at Chungking Mansion, workers at Midnight Express) more or less aestheticized.

The absent monumental space and blocks of residential buildings, the merely perceived and the lived space, suggest that what fascinates the director-*flâneur*'s footage and footsteps is the space in between the "slums" and skyscrapers, i.e., "the erotic spaces of pleasure and encounter" in Abbas's words (1997: 86). As mentioned earlier, Wong intends to provide through his film an artistic and authentic document of Hong Kong's urban spectacle by taking his audience to a path less trodden; as a result, images of the gorgeous, commercial space of Hong Kong are replaced by those of storefronts at a decayed building, undistinguished apartments, and cheap fast-food joints.[8] Seen from Lefebvre's scheme of urban morphology, *Chungking Express* only characterizes selected sites from two of the three major functions of urban spaces: meeting space such as "intermediate spaces for arteries, transitional areas, and places of business" (M), and private spaces such as houses and apartments (P).[9] The missing piece in the picture is the G (global) space, "the level of the system which has the broadest extension — namely the 'public' level of temples, palaces and political and administrative buildings" (155). *Chungking Express* avoids not only shots of the official global space (religious and political) as Lefebvre defines it, but also the spatial configurations that have emerged to accommodate the demands of the global capital flows such as the monumental buildings in Central, the fancy shopping arcades, the international franchised hotels, or the multinational office buildings. The airport and the restaurant California at Lan Kwai Fong appear as the only locus of global space, places which more often than not frustrate the walkers.

On the one hand, the invisible global space works in tune with the walkers' experience of the city — the picture-perfect global space lies outside of the everyday reality of those lower-middle class walkers on the street. The urban spectacle that attracts international investors and tourists might be physically close to the walkers but is virtually intangible to them in their daily experience of walking in the city. The cops that patronize the street market eatery and Midnight Express find more comfort in convenience stores than in the magnificent shopping arcades. The discrepancy between the cheated heroin smuggler's way of accumulating transnational capital and that of those who work for an international investment company in Hong Kong is as drastic as the differences between Chungking Mansion and any of the magnificent capitalist buildings such as the HSBC Headquarters. Similarly, the natural habitat of a fast-food joint helper like Faye will not be the enclave of fancy hotels or grandiose office buildings. It makes perfect sense given the class of the walkers in the film that the spectacular remains invisible on a daily basis. This phenomenon of "not seeing what is there," a reverse hallucination employed by Abbas to describe Hong Kong's cultural space as one of disappearance, here speaks for a dual vision of the city. The absent global space mirrors a realistic dimension of the ordinary Hong Kong walkers' experience of the metropolis — the invisible zone thereby suggests the boundaries in the polarized city. The visible global space in the film, namely the airport and the fashionable restaurant California, spells spaces of frustration and loss more than anything else for the walkers. The blonde-wigged walker loses her Indian partners at the airport; 633's first date with Faye at California ends up a lonely trip for both. Wong's alternative treatment of Hong Kong's much-publicized image of the dazzling "Pearl of the Orient," a capital showcase displaying nothing but spectacle and fantasy, offers "reasonable doubts" of the official account of the city. The effects on the walkers' everyday space felt through the power of the dual compression further suggests the way we think about the global city and its alleged concomitant free, open space. The material boundaries of the urban infrastructures can be transgressed but not erased by the pedestrians' uncontrollable footsteps. Specifically, the sense of freedom derived through such transgression is as ephemeral and illusory as that brought about by carnival, a safety valve that allows temporary subversion of the hierarchy of society only to maintain the stability of the social order.

The invisible monumental space in *Chungking Express* testifies eloquently to the imposed spatial barriers for the lower-middle class walkers in the film, an inevitable consequence of the polarized global city with a minority of high-paid white collars opposing the majority of ordinary walkers. Yet it is arguable if Wong's resistance to the ideology of progress embedded in the grand narrative of globalization is a conscious critique of contemporary Hong Kong. In fact, the absent dual city in the film can also point to the director-*flâneur*'s detached gaze, which results in a blind spot in the seemingly encompassing and omniscient mapping. Unsurprisingly, the director is more obsessed with walking and exploring the hidden corners of the city than with providing a harsh social critique of the spectacular or the abject, the conflicting urban space in a global city. In this sense, Wong retains the quintessential attribute of the classical *flâneur*'s detachment from the urban spectacle:

> The *flâneur*, according to Benjamin, takes the urban scene as a spectacle, strolling through it as though it were a diorama, that is, detached from involvement with its practical concerns and purposes. In making public places into playgrounds, the *flâneur* takes advantage of the systems of public order and control, and of production, which permit him to stroll safely and be entertained by the human comedy. (Weinstein and Weinstein 59-60)

In other words, the gaze of the *flâneur* can be compassionate, invested, and inquiring and at the same time detached, alienated, and passive.[10] It is the *flâneur*'s fascination with the spaces of encounter and the connections made possible by walking that renders some conspicuous global compression unseen and the representation of local compression (foreign labor or housing problem) inadequate. Like the character Faye in his film, Wong plays with the boundaries between the public and the private. As an heir to the Baudelairean *flâneur*, Wong turns the urban spectacle into a playground ready to entertain and be entertained by the shows of his walkers, their dreams and fears, hopes and frustrations — this explains why the tone of the film is both melancholy and light-hearted.

While Wong's treatment of the global city in *Chungking Express* suggests ways to reconsider the new myth of globalization and its mirage-like spaces, the film also ironically confirms the power of globalization as omnipresent and over-determining in the everyday life of the urban masses in Hong Kong. Similar to global capital's attempt to infiltrate every corner of the world, Wong strives to walk to every corner of the city. As discussed earlier, to a large extent, walking in Hong Kong as represented in *Chungking Express* registers a cycle of yearning and frustration due to the optimistic conception of their global city as brimming with possibilities and freedom. Polls in 1980s showed that Hong Kong residents considered their city "a land full of opportunities" despite the fact that "Hong Kong's economic success under a *laissez-faire* policy did not trickle down to reach each and every member of the community fairly" (Lau 80–1). The myth that globalization necessarily guarantees a prosperous future is implanted in the consciousness of many people in Hong Kong.[11] Given that the spatial configurations calibrated to global flows become daily realities in life, hardly can anyone be detached from the global dream.[12] In fact, it is fair to argue that the "repressed" G space in *Chungking Express* dominates and defines every walker's experience to a large extent: the invisible is omnipresent.[13] In *Chungking Express* the elusive global space, the hidden source that over-determines the spatial practice of walking in Hong Kong, partly accounts for the underlying drift of urbanites' emotions, rendering their pain and fears unspeakable, desires and pleasure uncertain. The *flâneur* in a global city is like Tantalus, caught between prohibitions and possibilities under the time-space compression.[14]

PART TWO

Between Global Flows and Carnal Flows:
Walking in Tokyo

> The power of a landscape does not derive from the fact that it offers itself as a spectacle, but rather from the fact that, as mirror and mirage, it presents any susceptible viewer with an image at once true and false of a creative capacity which the subject (or Ego) is able, during a moment of marvellous self-deception, to claim as his own.
>
> Henri Lefebvre

> I was born and grew up in Tokyo, so I grew up with those buildings. I was small, and buildings were small at first. Then buildings became bigger as I grew up. That strange intimacy with the buildings and the city is analogous to the mixed feelings for the parents: affections and fears are two sides of the same coin.
>
> Shinya Tsukamoto

This part of the book looks at the relationships among walking, violence, and globalization in Tokyo. I will juxtapose the representation of space of Tokyo, the official account of an efficient, affluent informational city of the future, with representational space, the private account dramatizing walking in Tokyo in Shinya Tsukamoto's films *Tetsuo: The Iron Man* series and *Tokyo Fist*. In this social/urban account, I will examine some significant urban restructuring projects during Tokyo's formation into a global city in the 1980s to demonstrate how the Tokyo metropolis invites its inhabitants to identify with the city's new image and find their sense of self firmly anchored in it. In other words, the global city prescribes a model relationship between the inhabitants and the capitalist space to its best advantage. In this sense, Tokyo is Henri Lefebvre's capitalist abstract space *par excellence*, which promotes flexible accumulation of capital at the cost of the inhabitants' everyday-life space by means of mimesis. Following Plato's use of mimesis as a means of aesthetic education for the elite class, imposing models for the guardians to emulate so as to reproduce ideal social relations, Lefebvre employs the term to elucidate the predicament facing the occupants of the abstract space. According to Lefebvre, the operative logic of abstract space is twofold: elevated subjectivity and civic consciousness shaped by the global city are inextricably bound up with the abstraction of the bodily experiences of the city-users. Deprived of the space of the body, the city-user becomes a body in an ever fragmentary space, a space that reduces the totality of life to the visual. With an emphasis on the function and effects of mimesis, my discussion of the urban plans and assorted building projects of Tokyo in the 1980s aims to show the model subject position projected for Tokyoites to emulate by urban plans and the construction boom, both as instruments of abstract space. The ideal inhabitants of the new Tokyo are defined as proud users of the global city even if their concrete space of everyday life becomes compressed and abstracted at a galvanizing speed. In short, in abstract space the conceived space overrides the concrete space of everyday life.

Ohkawabashi River City 21, a housing project built in 1986 by the Tokyo Metropolitan Housing Supply Corporation for those who gave up their no-longer-affordable living space in central Tokyo to make room for office space, shows how the violence of abstract space contains the conflicts it engenders. Forced to leave their homes under the pressure of rising rent and property tax or the maneuver of land purchase agencies, a large number of downtown residents moved to Ohkawabashi River City 21.[1] As the name of the project suggests, the composite of two high-rise towers and seven other medium-scaled residential buildings builds a miniature city in itself, a city ready for the twenty-first century. To maintain the affinity between the residents and the city center psychologically and physically, a new bridge was built for the residents of the 1,330 apartments to walk to work in central Tokyo, to serve the global city after the urban plans of rezoning marginalized them to the hinterland (Tajima 88).[2] The bridge to some extent works as an umbilical cord that ties the citizens in the suburbs to the global space. Moreover, all apartments provide impressive panoramic views of Tokyo. The spectacle of the dazzling city experienced through the gaze becomes an extension of the highly compartmentalized apartment of the public housing. No matter how tiny and parceled the apartment is, the inhabitant can look out from the window and see Tokyo, the whole city apparently always in sight and available in the eye of the beholder.[3] The spatial relations between the residents and the buildings demonstrate how the carrots-and-sticks trick compromises the lived space and how the inhabitants' living experience is dominated by the visual. Gradually losing the space of the body to answer the acute demands of capitalist space, the inhabitant of such a high-rise beehive turns to a body in space, or more precisely, a body contained in a space within numerous sub-divisions of spaces. Nonetheless, the ideology of homogeneity prevails over such a dispersed space: a big building in a global city creates for the inhabitants a sense of belonging to an ever-expanding and intact space.

In this part, Chapter 4 is devoted to exposing the invisible violence of

Tokyo's abstract space, while Chapter 5 seeks to critique the normalizing power of mimesis by exploring mimicry, a possible aberrational response to abstract space. I will draw on Roger Caillois's theory of mimicry to explain how the films of Shinya Tsukamoto, one of the most interesting contemporary Japanese directors, demonstrate the relationships among mimicry, subjectivity, and space under the domination of the global economy. If mimesis is the key to comprehending the violence of the homogenizing abstract space, mimicry, I would argue, registers an imaginary pathological consequence of this overriding abstract space. Caillois in his seminal article on mimicry uses facts about mimetic insects to demystify psychasthenia, a psychological disorder in which people confuse the space defined by the coordinates of their body with the represented space (Gregory 154). That is, they blur the boundaries between themselves and their surroundings. Caillois sees the living organism's imitation of the environment so as to blend in as a result of being seduced by the powerful space.

The theory of mimicry helps to explain how the subject can be so overwhelmed by and attracted to the power of abstract space that he becomes one with that space by mimicking the forces imposed on him, as seen in Tsukamoto's films. Presenting violence as an escalating fever against the backdrop of contemporary Tokyo, Tsukamoto articulates Tokyoites' oscillation between an intimate relationship with the city and an attempt to strike back against its inscrutable power. The picture-perfect global city with its concrete-and-steel buildings and virtual space of flows undergoes a transformation in the artistic representations into a postindustrial dehumanized space with forlorn walkers haunting the streets. The *Tetsuo* series and *Tokyo Fist* describe the hidden desire of an amenable salaryman to make his body as strong as the newly constructed high-rises everywhere in the city. Surrealistic to varying degrees, all of these films take place in a technology-obsessed Tokyo against the background of either a quiet suburban neighborhood or gleaming skyscrapers, both witnessing the violent metamorphosis of the salaryman's body into a killing machine. In these works, Tokyo signifies a wild kinetic field for the flows of primal desires and fears as well as for global flows. The pathological violence permeating the images of walkers and their walking invites us to consider the effects of the imposing global space.

Superimposing the urban geography of Tokyo redrawn by globalization and the artistic representation of contemporary Tokyo, one finds that the spatial relations between the subject and the global city constantly oscillating between mimesis and mimicry. Walking in abstract space on the one hand is a daily practice that enables the subject's identification with the city. However, this everyday bodily movement also registers a strategic site between the body and the city, a switch plate that might trigger all kinds of carnal flows in the walker, imitating the violence they bear on daily basis. As a spatial practice, walking designates the functional movement of a docile body, and simultaneously a reservoir of carnal energies assimilated into the oppressive space, waiting to be released in the same logic of the hostile surrounding.

4
Mimesis:
The Violence of Space

Abstract Space *Par Excellence*: Global/Fragmentary Space of Tokyo

Exploring Tokyo's urban morphology restructured by globalization in the 1980s and its ensuing violence, I contend that the problem with abstract space is its intrinsic violence, omnipresent but invisible. In this aspect, Lefebvre's theorization of abstract space as both normalizing and pathogenic will be particularly helpful for our exploration of Tokyo's cityscape redrawn in the context of global city construction. Specifically, the official urban plans and various high-rises built during the governmental, corporate, and residential construction boom of the 1980s in Tokyo show how the subjectivity of the city-user is boosted at the cost of repressed bodily experiences. I will present some concrete examples taken from Tokyo's global space and Lefebvre's theory of metonymy and metaphor, two major types of mimesis that define spatial relationships to see how mimesis, a normative code imposing violence on the body, constructs an instrumental subjectivity subservient to global capital flows.

The 1980s saw a drastic spatial restructuring of metropolitan Tokyo. This is the bubble era of Japan, in which the ubiquitous and colossal urban restructuring, initiated by a seemingly insatiable demand for office space for global capital flows, surrenders Tokyoites' everyday life to the "capitalist-friendly" space to an unparalleled extent. During this period, one could argue that all of the urban spatial elements become subordinate to the overriding order of globalization. From official pamphlets to actual enactment of urban plans, from corporate buildings to the New City Hall and the Bauhaus-style suburban housing projects, the Tokyo metropolis was cut up, sold, purchased, and utilized piece by piece to expedite the accumulation of capital. The urban restructuring cuts and slices Tokyo into the material sites of capital flows. As a result, Tokyoites are instructed to identify with the global city despite the fact that the centralization of the city not only places affordable housing 50 miles away from their workplaces but also shrinks their living space rapidly. If one comes to think of this history as a massive relocation project, desirable for Tokyoites or not, the violence of the restructuring is apparent and far-reaching.

Here Lefebvre's formulation of abstract space helps explain the logic of Tokyo urban development and the detrimental consequence to the inhabitants. Exploring the relationships among global capital, urbanization, and subject construction in *The Production of Space*, Lefebvre observes that global capital and urban restructuring go hand in hand to create what he calls abstract space, a space that reduces everything to serve the flexible accumulation. Such an instrumental space of exchange value becomes particularized, segregated, and broken so as to create a new order or homogeneity: the goal of flexible accumulation (Lefebvre 355–7). The process of cutting up, retailing, and segregating the urban space involves all kinds of violence as we see in Tokyo's urban redevelopment. The coalition of assorted interest groups including the private sectors such as land owners, construction companies, real estate agencies, the multinational capitalists, and the public sectors such as the Tokyo Metropolitan Government and the Liberal Democratic Party, manipulate the subdivision of space to serve their respective needs. At the same time, a homogenizing ideology is imposed on the carved-up space to annihilate differences and contradictions imminent to rezoning. For example, ordinary citizens living in the Central Business District area are forced to move out of the city center to make room for office space. They are unwitting participants in Tokyo's restructuring but denied the right to decide the subdivision of their own city.

Compromising or crushing everyday life for the purpose of capital flows, abstract space registers the brutal control of the rationally conceived space over the lived one and simultaneously conceals its own manipulative nature by inflicting a sense of homogeneity on the broken space. A simple rationale will be like this: the cutting up of the city is for the common good of all Tokyoites since a more important and affluent world city will ultimately benefit all its users. Simply put, violence is the inner logic of abstract space. As Derek Gregory elaborates,

> [c]apitalist and neocapitalist space is a space of quantification and growing homogeneity, a merchandized space where all the elements are exchangeable and thus interchangeable; a police space in which the state tolerates no resistance and no obstacles. *Economic space and political space thus converge towards the elimination of all differences.* (402; emphasis mine)

Abstract space means the production of the state and capital, working together to facilitate money flows.

Significantly, the collaboration of capital and urban restructuring cannot be sustained without a pedagogy of subject construction; that is, the space of globalization demands that the metropolis serve as concrete sites for capital accumulation, and the city requires its inhabitants as human resources to make the city-machine operate smoothly. Again, Lefebvre shrewdly observes that how one perceives and responds to the abstract space of globalization is achieved through an aesthetic process of mimesis, by imitating role models to become good copies (309). Mimesis dictates a model for the subject as space-users with autonomy and freedom, an elite position echoing Plato's standard guardian in the Republic. Like the political education of the guardian class, which aims to make the members perform appropriate duties for the state, mimetic subjects of abstract space should devote themselves to fulfilling tasks required by the global city. In other words, to enable the flows of global capital and simultaneously sustain stable social relationships, mimesis as an instrument of the ideal space defines proper relations between the subject and his or her surroundings, instructing one to interpret and perceive the social reality. For Lefebvre, mimesis is what conceals the violence of abstract space, which prioritizes capital over the occupants of the space.[1] The potential guardians of the state are socialized from childhood to imitate only that which will contribute to their future role as the privileged of the society and avoid whatever is detrimental to this role. By the same token, the model subject of abstract space has to ensure an appropriate spatial relationship by repressing irrational desires. It is precisely the designated elite bearings that enslave the occupant of the space to flexible accumulation, repressing the concrete everyday life, the sensory/sexual experiences of the subject.

Global City Tokyo: An Official Story

In the discourse of Tokyo's urban planning we find vivid examples of mimesis as an instrument projecting an ideal subject-position with which one can identify. In the prime time of the bubble years, urban planners ask Tokyoites to adapt to changes for a city of tomorrow. The urban plan proposed by the National Commission on Land Development in 1986 exemplifies the official version of the global city formation campaign:

> Presently, as the rapid trend of transformation into a world city increases an already excessive demand for office space, Tokyo is facing many new problems, such as the rising price of land in central areas. Greater supply of space, urban restructuring, better urban infrastructures and living conditions are among the tasks to be carried out. (Machimura 1998: 183)

Archetypal of Tokyo's urban planning in the 1980s, this proposal suggests that while achieving the goal of Tokyo as a global city, relocation of the observed over-concentrated city population is urgently needed.

From what we witness a decade later in the 1990s, this planning discourse is carried out to its full extent. It is therefore necessary to go back to examine closely how a mass consent is reached to achieve such a mammoth urban redevelopment project. The land use plan, a pertinent example of the ideal Tokyo promoted by its urban planners, brings to realization Lefebvre's definition of abstract space. As an abstract space *par excellence*, Tokyo requires its inhabitants to provide "greater supply of space," for example, by giving up one's home at the city center and moving to suburban housing. Lefebvre constantly emphasizes the duplicity of the global space, its ability to claim inhabitants as the proud users of the space and at the same time deprive them of the capacity to master their own lived space. How the population in central Tokyo should be relocated is obviously not the stated concern in the urban plan; the goal of modernization alone justifies the means of urban rezoning. What makes the restructuring possible is the mimesis of the subject-position implied by the urban planning. As the Land Development plan exemplifies, promoting and promising better living conditions, the official document suggests citizens as an essential participant of the grand plan of constructing a world city.

Such logic of changing living conditions for the sake of a future of global city is articulated in Suzuki Shunichi's project of realizing the ideal of "My Town Tokyo" as the twin of "World City Tokyo." In fact, the long-reigning patriarch governor of Tokyo from 1979 to 1995 has been vigorously advocating the concept of "My Town Tokyo" as his central guideline of urban plans since 1981. From then on, in almost every official publication of Tokyo Metropolitan Government, Suzuki promulgates the idea of celebrating a global city that remains a "town that one can call one's home." Juxtaposing these two slogans as two sides of the same coin, Suzuki, like Land Development bureaucrats, encourages the citizens to identify with Tokyo as a town retrieving a sense of community, and as a global city in the making:

> The words "my town" may have a tone of intimacy that may seem rather incongruous with one of the world's biggest cities, Tokyo. But this tone of intimacy is considered the very key point in envisioning the future of Tokyo. In the past, the trend was that in the bigger city, the more tenuous the relationship became between it and its residents. Roads have been opened, new buildings constructed and old buildings demolished one after another without the knowledge of the residents. The town that was once their own changes to an "unknown town" before they realized what was happening. . . . But the phrase "My Town Tokyo" amply reflects a concept of taking a renewed look at such a city from the standpoint of residents and retrieving it as truly their own. In this sense, it may be said that the "My Town Tokyo" concept represents an envisioning of the future of Tokyo from the standpoint of the residents and the local community. (3)

This passage from the preface of the *2nd Long-term Plan for the Tokyo Metropolis* shows how citizens are instructed to identify with the new Tokyo for the twenty-first century and in so doing to work together with the city government in the service of the global flows. The urban planners prescribe a role model for the new citizens of Tokyo to imitate, a resident who is fully aware of what is happening in the global city since the big metropolis is no more an unknown town but a familiar extension of one's local community. The tenuous relationship between the big city and its citizens is defined as outdated and undesirable; a model citizen for the city of the future should remain intimate with the ever-developing metropolis. Claiming Tokyo as "my town," one is drawn to the metropolis and expected to accept the fact that there will always be new roads opening, construction of new buildings and annihilation of old ones. The proposal suggests that the knowledge of the ongoing urban development is the key to the affinity between the inhabitants and their changing space: the new Tokyoites are informed and therefore ready for any change taking place in the city.

All the Glittering Buildings: You Are What You See

The 1980s are remembered as an era in which an unparallel construction boom extended from central Tokyo to its hinterlands. I intend to look into this construction boom and explore the dual logic of the Tokyo expansion. The urban architecture serves global capital not only as the material site of virtual flows but also as the agency that mediates the relation between the body and the space. As Sassen asserts, Tokyo owes its sudden rise to a world city to the fact that global capital requires concrete places to organize and extend economic activities (1991: 5). The concentration of international

Expressways and high-rise buildings: two important elements of the Global City.
(Picture taken in Akasaka, Tokyo, by Yen-bin Chiou in July 2003)

capital and labor further entails significant changes in the social, political, and cultural environments of such large cities. The logic of global flows dominates the lived space of the inhabitants and turns Tokyo into a truly abstract space. Again, abstract space renders its logic of violence invisible via mimesis: the high-rises, as conspicuous signs of power, guarantee that Tokyoites will identify with the glorious future of the city they embody and assume the role of an instrument for flexible accumulation. They are designated as autonomous users of the global space.

It is worth noting that the expansion of abstract space and its legitimacy established by mimesis cannot be comprehended without taking into consideration both the part (urban plans, rezoning, new buildings) and the whole (global city Tokyo) at the same time. I will focus on the Century Tower, the New City Hall, and the public housing Ohkawabashi River City 21. Each one represents a specific type of building constructed to meet different demands of the global city. The Century Tower is one among many corporate buildings that represent the core of the construction boom, directly brought about by the influx of global capital. The New City Hall for many reasons presented later in my discussion is Tokyo Metropolitan Government's attempt to claim local control of the changes resulted from capital globalization. The Ohkawabashi River City 21 is the suburban housing project that reveals the contradiction inherent in the retailing of Tokyo's urban space to promote the global flows. One witnesses how the inhabitants are relocated to the hinterland of Tokyo so as to make room for the office buildings in the city centers. Each of these three examples claims to provide Tokyoites the ownership of Tokyo in its own way, but taken together they show abstract space in the making and its consequent hidden violence on the concrete space of inhabitants' everyday life.

First of all, the construction frenzy in the 1980s powerfully testifies to the fragmentation and commercialization of Tokyo's urban space resulting from the globalization of the Japanese economy. With the appreciation of the yen and the emergence of Tokyo as a global financial center in the early 1980s, Tokyo attracted a huge influx both of Japanese and foreign corporate headquarters, financial institutions, and securities companies.[2] The keen shortage of office space created a collective need to meet the demands and make profits by re-developing Tokyo's urban structure. The National Land Agency's proposal estimates the upcoming demand for office space in central Tokyo to be more than 50 million square meters for the next 18 years to come (Machimura 1992: 118). In fact, the booming economy in the 1980s motivated every major construction company and real estate company to come up with its own imaginary urban plan to shape Tokyo as a city of tomorrow. The mushrooming office buildings in central Tokyo are indeed the city's answer to the great demand for office space.

Among the buildings constructed during the construction boom, the Century Tower located in east central Tokyo illuminates the spirit of the historical moment of the global era. This "intelligent" office building, typical of many other high-rises built in the same period of time, aims to "accommodate all the functions and services required by a computerised building in the foreseeable future" (Tajima 66). The Century Tower is a high-tech building in tune with the image of Tokyo as the city of the future. The architecture itself is an expression of globalization. A project completed in 1991, the building was designed by Sir Norman Foster, the English architect whose HSBC Headquarters became Hong Kong's new landmark and is recognized as a masterpiece of world architecture. Fascinated by the outstanding structure and the shining glass walls of HSBC Headquarters, the client for Century Tower requested Norman Foster to clone this monumental building for Tokyo. The outcome is "a scaled-down version," a 19 story twin towers separated by a central atrium (Tajima 66).

Paradoxically, National Commission's slogan of a "greater supply of space," returning space to the city for more building construction like the Century Tower, in fact always refers to what I shall describe as an emptying-out of the body. The body is decorporealized (abstracted) because on the one hand the stretching of the buildings greatly destroys the old living quarters and on the other hand this construction boom seeks to bring back the inhabitants psychologically with the spectacle of the global sublime as demonstrated by the buildings. As Lefebvre notes, abstract space is dominated by the eye and the gaze: "By the time the process [of decorporealization] is complete, our space has no social existence independently of an intense, aggressive and repressive visualization" (286). A global city like Tokyo is a space of signs. The flows of information and signs prevailing in such a space incline to subsume the flows of bodily desires and sensory impressions. That is, rather than corresponding to the needs of the beholder, the myriad images fashion the desires. The predominance of visual experience easily makes high-rises the embodiment of entrepreneur power by being tall and erect, a phallic symbol securing deference and admiration from the spectator. The predilection for the visual allows the spectator to relate to only two determinants of the building, the façade and the perpendicularity. Such a spatial relation between the body and the building boils down to nothing but a one-way gaze from the spectator. The prioritization of the visual thus brings about a constant metaphorization of the body: "[l]iving bodies, the bodies of 'users' — are caught up not only in the toils of parcellized space, but also in the web of... images, signs and symbols. *These bodies are transported out of themselves, transferred and emptied out, as it were, via the eyes...*" (Lefebvre 98; emphasis mine).

One might argue that those who work in a corporate building like the Century Tower find themselves relating to the building more than its verticality or the façade. Still, the salaryman who painstakingly commutes to work in a tiny space in the office building in central Tokyo is subjugated to the space by metonymy, another form of mimesis. According to Lefebvre, metonymy, in which a part refers to the whole, designates a "to-and-fro movement enforced with carrot and stick between the part and the whole." A perfect example of this logic is the occupants of a highly compartmentalized apartment or office building with "stack after stack of 'boxes for living in' ": "the spectator-*cum*-tenants grasp the relationship between part and whole directly; furthermore, they recognize themselves in that relationship. By constantly expanding the scale of things, this movement serves to compensate for the pathetically small size of each set of living quarters" (98). The corporate culture requires the employees to identify completely with the company in the manner of samurais to the feudal lords.[3] The affinity between the employees and the corporation that often guarantees life-long employment can easily be stretched to the material space of the corporations, the buildings in the business district of the city. "You are where you work": the lingering belief in judging how respectable a person is by the company he or she works for and how prestigious a company is by its address intensifies the employee's identification with the *kaisha* (company), the office building, and by extension with Tokyo, the habitat of the office building. The strong proclivity for the global sublime motivates the employees to willingly serve abstract space on a daily basis even though their office cubicle is never expanded and the paychecks somehow fail to catch up with the evident glory of the cityscape in sight everyday.

Those officials who work in the Tokyo Metropolitan Government can argue otherwise, raving about their office cubicle that does expand due to the construction boom. When the Tokyo Metropolitan Government shows its support for the construction rush by committing to the construction of a new office building, hardly any Tokyoites can stay psychologically removed from this global city formation campaign. The New City Hall is a complex of three interconnected structures with an extended "Citizens' Plaza" in front of the 48 story No. 1 tower (243 meters high) located in West Shinjuku and opened in 1991. The cluster of buildings occupies three full city blocks of approximately 14,349 square meters in one of the most expensive urban areas in the world.[4]

The New City Hall in West Shinjuku, Tokyo.
(Picture taken by Yen-bin Chiou in July 2003)

Completed under the influence of unconstrained economic ebullience, the New City Hall has been represented and advertised by the governor Suzuki as a space for the citizens from the very beginning. For example, one official reason for the Tokyo Metropolitan Government to move away from the Marunouchi administration area is to physically bring the government closer to the actual population center of the city, West Shinjuku. As the symbol of Tokyo as a world city, this dazzling new home of an ambitious government aims to "provide better services for the citizens" and "an arena for open and free exchanges among Tokyo residents" (Tokyo Metropolitan Government 1989: 74). In fact, Suzuki depicted the showpiece as "a gift for the metropolis' citizens of the 21st century" (Cybriwsky 155).

For the governor, the New City Hall is the mammoth project emblematic of the ideal composite of "My Town Tokyo" and "World City Tokyo," with the former intensifying the identification between the citizens and the metropolis and the latter the role of Tokyo as a nodal point of global flows. Specifically, the urban discourse states "the New City Hall will also function as a symbol of the 'International City Tokyo' to expand international exchanges along with the increasing importance of international exchanges at the citizen and local government level. Moreover, it will also serve as a symbol of 'Home Town Tokyo' and strongly enhance the hometown consciousness of the citizens . . . " (Tokyo Metropolitan Government 1987: 267). The construction history of the New City Hall and the design of the buildings thus typify a crowning monument built in the name of the citizens to address the political and economic symbolism of a specific historical moment.[5]

The Tokyo Metropolitan Government's "My Town Tokyo" concept that works to construct a new identity of Tokyoites at the global era is materialized in the New City Hall. This monumental building crystallizes how the images of the architecture can become a means of political education to construct Tokyoites' subjectivity in proportion to the expansion of the global city. To justify the construction of this new building, Tokyo Metropolitan Government resorts to the importance of realizing the ideal of "My Town Tokyo" for citizens to cope with changes of the urban space at the turn of the century. The second long-term plan of Tokyo prescribes that "[t]he Tokyo Metropolitan Government (TMG) is taking steps to realize the 'My Town Tokyo' concept vigorously so that all citizens can cope with such enormous changes and pass on the city in favorable condition to the next generation" (267). Again, the appropriate subject-position is a citizen capable of adapting to the new metropolis with the help of the government. For all the sweeping urban changes, new Tokyoites should find the city "a nice town" to inhabit. Such ideal citizens will then serve as role models for future Tokyoites to emulate.

The exterior of the New City Hall may well be paradigmatic of the monumental building, which addresses an implied agent with its spatial logic: a postmodern montage of Notre-Dame style Edo castle[6] and computer chips, a symbol of aspiring to the future of the city by recalling its past. Kenzo Tange, the architect of the project, explained the concept of the façade:

> [t]he lattice-like pattern of windows, and of marble and granite on the exterior of the buildings, was intended to invoke the memory of geometric timber-frame buildings of Edo as well as the circuit board of a computer, an apt metaphor for the age of information and technology in Tokyo over which these government headquarters now preside. (Coaldrake 272)

The New City Hall's resemblance to the Edo castle makes a spatial statement that sees the booming present and the promising future of Tokyo as an extension of its glorious past, clearly signified by samurais' residences. If the spectacular skyscrapers hint at a contemporary version of the castle, who can be a more qualified user of that space than the modern samurai, the middle class Tokyoites like the salaryman?[7]

Under the spell of the monumental space, which seems to be always expanding and yet highly accessible, the city-users are tempted to identify with the spatial center of power, part of the matrix of global city transformation. They are encouraged to enjoy vicariously the sublime power demonstrated by the new monumental buildings whose conception and construction invite them to claim the urban space as their domain so as to justify the political and economic purposes of the buildings. The official representation of Shinjuku as a rising star in Japan with its new landmark, the New City Hall complex, will not present the interpretation of the skyscrapers as more a monument to the governor himself or to the architect Kenzo Tange than the people of Tokyo.[8] Nor does the choice of the location of the towers appear to the citizens as motivated by making the sub-center Shinjuku a worthy competitor with the prestigious Marunouchi to attract the headquarters of big companies and further the accumulation of capital. Likewise, the official narrative of the New City Hall is telling a different story of the project from those who critique the complex as the "Tax Tower," indicating its expenses, and the "Tower of Bubble," constructed not with granite and marble but the bubbles of the 1980s' buoyant economy (Cybriwsky 155). The myth of endless economic growth, as prophetic as it is tangible by a glance at the monumental buildings of the New City Hall, produces an illusory space for the inhabitants, fostering a proud identification with "My Town Tokyo." The question is: can the increasing compression of everyday living space be compensated for by a mere look at the spectacular New City Hall or a walk in the Citizens' Plaza?

One manifest reason for monumental buildings like the Century Tower or the New City Hall to maintain a stable imaginary relationship between the grand global city and its users is the construction of public housing projects in the suburban areas. Those people who directly confront the effective violence wrought by rezoning, those who are forced to move out of the central wards, need more than the glittering image composed by the buildings to call the global city their home. They need a reason to justify why their residence falls outside of their control. Suburban housing projects like Ohkawabashi

River City 21 are the carrots that serve to alleviate the pain brought about by the centralization of Tokyo, the antidote to the conflicts of spatial apartheid which cannot be taken care of by mere slogans like "My Town Tokyo equals World City Tokyo." Seen in this light, public housing designates the by-product of the office/governmental buildings, another infrastructure to hold a tighter rein on the mimetic relationship between the body and the city.

Notably, the Bauhaus-style Ohkawabashi River City 21 is adjacent to the traditional local housing of Tsukuda-jima, a not-yet-globalized fisherman's island. A local from the Tsukuda-jima describes his experience of "looking down on the neighbours" (Ohkawabashi River City 21) as seeing "another town and another world" (Tajima 88). The contrast, like Hong Kong's Lantau Island, a traditional village transformed to the home of Disneyland, has been regarded as a perfect example of a "contradictory city," a hybrid of the modern and the tradition. Yet the contradictions imbued in such a hybrid space conceal the contradictory nature of space as both fragmentary and global, as elucidated by the spatial relationships between the indoctrinated inhabitants and the residential buildings.

One crucial contradiction of Tokyo as an abstract space is revealed through the spatial relationship between Tokyo and the millions of suburban inhabitants who cannot simply walk across a bridge to the city center or admire the skyline at home. They have to commute everyday to see part and parcel of "My Town Tokyo" and work for their city of the future. The commuting nightmare that haunts millions of Tokyoites is one of the most glaring consequences of the prioritization of office over residential space. The centralization of capital and information flows in central Tokyo parallels the marginalization of an increasing number of ordinary citizens to its hinterland requiring an average 1 to 2 hours one way commuting to the city centers such as CBD or Shinjuku.[9] More than 7 million passengers use the subway system daily.[10] The amazing number of commuters accounts for the fully packed rush-hour train ride, yet we can hardly imagine a physically painful ride due to the maximum compression of the human body. A close look at the subway employees with white gloves gives a better idea of the hellish congestion in the subway train. It might not be stated clearly in their job description, yet one of these subway employees' major responsibilities every morning during the rush hour is to push in those passengers who cannot get their whole body or belongings to fit into the subway car, so the door can close. A human version of a sardine can is indeed an understatement.[11] In a sense, the overcrowded subway train stands for the container that disciplines the bodies of the commuters for the global city they head for. Before one feels at home in the city upon seeing "My Town Tokyo," one's body has to undergo violence brought about by the literal compression of space. Commuting thus spells the mimesis at work to the point of physically disciplining the subjects.

5
From Mimesis to Mimicry:
Memory, Subjectivity, and Space

As demonstrated above, mimesis is crucial to the conception of official urban planning and the assorted construction projects that cater to the demands of globalization in Tokyo. It serves as a looking glass held up by abstract space for its occupants to see themselves as an indispensable part of an ever-prosperous global city. Nevertheless, this looking glass is treacherous: abstract space appears subservient to the subjects but in fact its users are manipulated to serve the flows of global capital. Appearing analogous to the Lacanian mirror stage, which promises the formation of the subjectivity, this mirror that reflects the image of the self is as deceptive as that of Snow White's stepmother and as tricky as Alice's looking glass. As Lefebvre insightfully points out, "For space offers itself like a mirror to the thinking 'subject', but, after the manner of Lewis Carroll, the 'subject' passes through the looking-glass and becomes a lived abstraction" (313–4). The magic mirror on the wall that always attempts to assure the already indoctrinated subject as an eligible user of the space constantly seduces the looker to walk into the looking-glass to become a strange hybrid of elevated subjectivity and evacuated body, trained to see fragments as whole.

If mimesis explains the "norm-bound" nature of the urban space of Tokyo in the 1980s, I would contest this normalizing formation by critically reading

---

This chapter is developed from the author's article "Tetsuo: Salaryman or Iron Man?" posted on line in the special edition of Asian cinema review in *Scope* (2003) (http://www.nottingham.ac.uk/film/journal/filmrev/films-asian-cinema.htm).

into the abstract space of Tokyo the possibilities of its malfunction. Again, abstract space is both norm-bound and pathogenic. The tension between the expanding global space of flows and the lived space, the space embedded in fixed material conditions, results in a bodily unconscious. The repressed concrete space of everyday life, the space of the sensory and the sensual of city-users, becomes the unconscious that often returns in the form of powerful kinetic physical energies, a struggle of the body long subjugated to the violence of the rationally conceived abstract space. The following discussion examines a situation when mimesis slips into a state of duality in which the subjects both follow the norms of the dominant spatial matrix to sustain their subjectivity and paradoxically are drawn to the space to the point of erasing their subjectivity to become one with their surroundings. In such a case the subjects are so overwhelmed by the sublime built environment of abstract space as embodied by the buildings and urban infrastructure that they tend to integrate with the space of contemporary capitalism. This pathogenic phenomenon can be best described as mimicry, one of the possible aberrational consequences of the violence of abstract space and indeed a most revealing one. Reflecting not only the demands of mimesis but also its failure as an instrument of producing a useful and docile body, mimicry marks a point of departure from which we can examine critically the violence of abstract space.

As a term from biological studies, mimicry designates a survival strategy of "superficial resemblance of two or more organisms that are not closely related taxonomically." "This resemblance confers an advantage — such as protection from predation — upon one or both organisms through some form of 'information flow' that passes between the organism and the animate agent of selection" (*Encyclopedia Britannica* 144). The best example is the phasmids, or so-called stick insects and leaf insects. To blend in perfectly with their surroundings, foliage-eating stick insects have evolved to look and move as the plants that they inhabit to avoid attention from potential predators. To survive violence from the external environment, phasmids efface their subjectivity, disappearing in the space so as to show up somewhere else alive. Such mimicry, functioning as camouflage, differs from the way a chameleon protects itself by temporarily changing its colors. The stick insects' morphology and behavior have evolved to be part of their environment. Interestingly, according to Roger Caillois, a defense mechanism is an insufficient reason to explain why mimetic species mingle with their surroundings (65). For example, scientists prove that "resemblance is in the eye of the beholder" (Caillois 61). Predators of the mimetic insects are not fooled by the trick.

Sparrows, for instance, feed on the crickets or phasmids that completely simulate twigs, leaves or small stones, invisible to the human eyes (Caillois 66). In some cases, mimicry is a defense mechanism that backfires. Gardeners destroy the caterpillars of the geometer-moth while pruning the shoots of shrubbery, which they so successfully resemble. Phyllia, another mimetic insect, simulates the foliage to such an extent that they cannot tell another Phyllia from the leaves they feed on. The sad result is a kind of "collective masochism": they devour each other because of their mimicry, a "defense-mechanism" that goes too far (Caillois 67).

This biological understanding is instructive in our explorations of the relationships between subjectivity and space. Caillois, although not a Lefebvrian scholar himself, provides insightful observations for us to engage in a full-scale analysis of the detrimental consequences of abstract space suggested by Lefebvre. Starting with the biological phenomenon of the mimicry of living creatures, Caillois delves into the dynamics between subjectivity and space in an effort to explain the relationships between mimicry and psychasthenia, or a subject's disorientation in space. Caillois postulates that mimicry indicates the individual's seduction by space, a process of assimilation that is "necessarily accompanied by a decline in the feeling of personality and life" (72). The waning affect that defines mimicry, the disappearing boundaries between the body and the milieu, results from the domination of the scientifically represented space over the individually perceived space (the conceived space vs. the lived space). Deprived of the privilege as the "origin of the coordinates," one is reduced to nothing more than one point among others. Unable to map out the surroundings with the immediacy of the body, the subject becomes disoriented. As a consequence, the subject in space is unable to differentiate his or her corporeality from the external environment. This is what Caillois means by "depersonalization by assimilation": "[t]he feeling of personality, considered as the organism's feeling of distinction from its surroundings, of the connection between consciousness and a particular point in space, cannot fail under these conditions to be seriously undermined . . . " (70, 72).

Caillois compares the dislocated subject's assimilation into the space to schizophrenics' disturbed perception of himself in relation to the space: "*I know where I am, but I do not feel as though I'm at the spot where I find myself*" (72). The schizophrenic's typical response to the question "Where are you?" helps us better understand not only the conflicts between corporeality and subjectivity, lived space and conceived space, but also the mimic relation between the body and the space:

> To these dispossessed souls, space seems to be a devouring force. Space pursues them, encircles them, digests them in a gigantic phagocytosis. It ends by replacing them. Then the body separates itself from thought, the individual breaks the boundary of his skin and occupies the other side of his senses. He tries to look at *himself from* any point whatever in space. He feels himself becoming space, *dark space where things cannot be put.* He is similar, not similar to something, but just *similar.* (72; emphasis original)

Subsumed by the forces of the space, the subject cannot see the power but always feels it. When the power of the space becomes too overwhelming, the subject tends to be drawn to the enveloping environment and to depersonalization, the effect of falling for the space in the way iron is attracted to a magnet. The ultimate ambivalence of mimicry lies in the fact that self-defense and self-denial are two sides of the same coin: while the living creature survives by expanding into its surroundings, "life seems to lose ground, blurring in its retreat the frontier between the organism and the milieu . . . " (Caillois 74). Mimicry thus describes a paradoxical relationship between the organism and its surroundings — the living creature is attracted to the space that devours it. Such a self-preservation mechanism simultaneously points to an instinct of renunciation that "orients it toward a mode of reduced existence, which in the end would no longer know either consciousness or feeling . . . " (74). Seen in this light, Caillois's mimicry is neither conscious resistance as Homi Bhabha endorses nor merely a defense mechanism as it is generally defined.[1]

The theorization of mimicry brings to light a possible interaction between subject and space: suppressed and tempted by the power of abstract space, the subject ends up mimicking the surrounding environment, acting and looking like the space he or she inhabits. Experiencing the spatial violence of decorporealization on a daily basis, the subject mimics an absolute power, whose source remains unseen, by reducing him or herself to assimilate into the environment and exerting violence on the body.

Salaryman or Iron Man? *Tetsuo: The Iron Man* and *Tetsuo II: Body Hammer*

The relationships among mimicry, subjectivity, and space are dramatized in Shinya Tsukamoto's Tokyo films including the *Tetsuo (The Iron Man)* series and *Tokyo Fist*, which present mimicry as a pathological symptom in abstract space. Produced in the late 1980s and early 1990s, these three films established

Tsukamoto's international reputation as one of the best Japanese film makers of his generation. Winning the Grand Prize at the Rome International Fantastic Film Festival for his debut 35 mm film, *Tetsuo: The Iron Man*, Tsukamoto continues to inquire in his subsequent films[2] not only the interactions between the human body and inorganic materials but also into the conundrum of living in Tokyo facing the twenty-first century. These films all center on the metamorphosis of an archetypal salaryman character into a fierce fighter. The protagonists' act of taking on an arsenal body can be interpreted as a malfunctioning mimesis of identity that slips into mimicry of the violent abstract space of the global city. In the following discussion, I will read Tsukamoto's *Tetsuo* series as sci-fi allegories of the subject's mimicking the violence of the city and further explore in detail how the dynamics between the body and the city is played out in his later work *Tokyo Fist*.

Tetsuo: The Iron Man (1989) and its sequel *Tetsuo II: Body Hammer* (1992), with their major characters literally becoming cyborgs, narrate how Tokyoites, attracted to the overwhelming power of the urban landscape composed of concrete and iron, mimic the urban landscape of Tokyo. A combination of Japanese *manga* and quasi-*Blade Runner* cyberpunk, the *Tetsuo* series tells the horror story of the salaryman's bodily transformation with minimal plot, provocative visual effects, and piercing industrial music.[3] Both films feature a mysterious fusion of metal and flesh which depersonalizes the salaryman, who comes to lose his subjectivity in order to merge with the space.

In *Tetsuo: The Iron Man*, the unnamed protagonist is first represented as just another agreeable salaryman in the city, whose carnal energies, repressed by the "clean and proper" space, can hardly be seen except in the wild sex between him and his sexy girlfriend.[4] Yet everything in his life is turned upside down after he runs over a young man on the street, a metal fetishist inserting iron into his body. Driving to a suburban area with his girlfriend, the salaryman hits this metal fetishist, who runs in frenzy at the sight of the rusted metal scrap in his own thigh infested with maggots. The couple, without realizing the consequences of this bizarre incident, have wild sex in the bushes, excited at the idea of the victim of the accident lying somewhere down the hill watching them making love. Not until the next day when the salaryman sees an iron thorn protruding out of his skin does he start to be aware of what the hit-and-run accident entails. With his flesh continuously evolving into metal, the horrified protagonist becomes more and more alienated from his salaryman identity (no salary and not a man). Later when he makes love to his girlfriend, the salaryman witnesses with great trepidation metal bursting out of his body with uncontrollable force. Ashamed of his grotesque body, he hides away from his girlfriend in a small corner of the house. The girlfriend's early response, "Show it to me. I don't get frightened easily," leads her to an unthinkable bloodbath. Little does she know that her boyfriend's body has become an unrecognizable mass piled up with metal debris. What is worse, his penis suddenly changes into a powerful electric drill. Horror-stricken, the girlfriend defends herself by stabbing the iron man but still fails to save herself from being penetrated and killed by the penis-turned-drill. The salaryman now realizes that he has irreversibly become a metal fetishist.

As the protagonist becomes more and more alienated from his own human flesh, he increasingly becomes part of the urban space he occupies, in terms of both the materials and its violence. Thus, the story of the iron man demonstrates in a classically expressionistic manner the violence of a global city, as if the salaryman could not see what the city truly is unless he also becomes abstract space itself. Not only is the protagonist forced to undergo a metamorphosis into a metal body; his environment, the global city Tokyo, also morphs into an abject space of horror and agony, with city crowds emerging as monsters from unknown lands. For example, on the way to his office the morning after spotting the iron sticking out from his face while shaving, the salaryman runs into an iron woman where he least expects to find one. This office lady, a female counterpart of the salaryman, is waiting for the train on a bench with the salaryman. Out of curiosity, she reaches for a deserted lump of metal on the ground of the subway station and soon becomes possessed by the rusted metal. All of a sudden, the transformed woman with metallic tentacles worse than Edward Scissorhands starts to assault the salaryman, chasing after him through the subway tunnels. A simple routine of walking in the city now turns to a dystopian fantasy of daily disasters.

To some extent, the metal that takes over the salaryman's body allegorizes the domination of the industrialized urban space. Instead of seeing a city of high-rises, we see the assorted convulsive images of metal for industrial use or construction. What makes contemporary Tokyo stages its presence in every possible realistic and fantastic form: from the metal and machine in the factory to the metals that invade every imaginable orifice of the human body. Taking on a form identical with the urban environment in materials, the unnamed protagonist fearfully and reluctantly becomes one with his habitat. The salaryman's transformation into an iron man in *Tetsuo: The Iron Man* is less mimicry than a critique of mimesis, the homogenizing forces that make citizens identify with abstract space. Both the unknown woman and the salaryman's experiences of changing progressively into a cyborg resemble a contagious disease, implying the subject's assimilation into the urban space as an uncontrollable contamination.

While *Tetsuo: The Iron Man* presents mimicry of the abstract space of Tokyo as a mishap of undesirable but irreversible metamorphosis, its sequel *Tetsuo II: Body Hammer* questions whether Tokyoites can escape from such a misfortune. In a sense, *Tetsuo II: Body Hammer* echoes Philip Dick's science fiction *Do Androids Dream of Electric Sheep*, which later became well known in the film adaptation, *Blade Runner*. Like Deckard, the protagonist in *Blade Runner*, the main character Tomoo in *Tetsuo II: Body Hammer* is tremendously confused, not knowing if the dehumanized surroundings he sees are part of the ordinary world or post-apocalyptic. Yet what distinguishes the two archetypes is the solution each chooses at the end of the film. The protagonist in *Blade Runner* decides to abandon the immediate environment to look for an idyllic alternative, but his Japanese counterpart opts for mimicking the steel-and-concrete environment so as to realize the dream of living in a pastoral space.

In *Tetsuo: The Iron Man*, the urban environment is presented through the expressionist lens; however, the object of mimicry is much more apparent and concrete in its sequel. The setting of Tokyo is highlighted in *Tetsuo II: Body Hammer*. The nightmarish lump of steel and iron rampant in the city in *Tetsuo: The Iron Man* appears as numerous high-rises compacted in the city in *Tetsuo II: Body Hammer*. The dazzling buildings that serve to define the ideal spatial relationship between the body and the city from the very beginning look oppressive and threatening to the protagonist. In other words, the abstract space of Tokyo takes an expressionist form of Fritz Lang's dehumanized skyscrapers in *Metropolis*. Buildings change from "clean and proper" space to sites of imminent danger and devilish violence. Again, reminiscent of the pursuit between Deckard and the android among the tops of skyscrapers in *Blade Runner*, Tomoo's chase after the cyborg-thugs induces acrophobia in the viewer. The pathological response to the altitude of the high-rise is the flip side of the phallic verticality, in contrast to the sense of power and sublime experienced by those who command the panoptic view from above as well as those who admire the phallic building from below.

Moreover, the sequel reverses the narrative of the first *Tetsuo*. To be precise, the story is not about the transformation of a nice-guy salaryman into a militant iron man as *Tetsuo: The Iron Man* describes but vice versa, and the daily walk in the city is in fact a strong repression symptomatic of abstract space. In appearance, *Tetsuo II: Body Hammer* narrates the same type of story of a salaryman becoming attracted to the urban space. Like *Tetsuo: The Iron Man*, the film starts with the depiction of a typical salaryman, Tomoo, leading a happy family life in Tokyo with his darling wife, Kana, and their young boy. The protagonist soon goes through a series of Kafkaesque events, each centering on a family member being kidnapped, twice his little boy, then himself and finally his wife. Similar to its predecessor, the sequel then shows how the salaryman's normal life in the city of Tokyo falls into pieces all of a sudden. However, as the plot unfolds, it turns out that the abduction of the family members is an attempt by the cyborg gang to bring back Tomoo to their tribe. Tomoo's long lost brother, the leader of the gang, attempts to awaken the dormant violence in his salaryman body, knowing that Tomoo has always been a cyborg but resists such an identity.

Such a twist on the original story of a salaryman allows the director to explore the tangled relationships among memory, subjectivity, and space. Tomoo's repressed memory of his cyborg identity reveals the mimesis of the salaryman's identity from a different, critical perspective. Instilled by their Frankenstein-like scientist father the gene of mutation to fight against a decaying world, both Tomoo and his brother can transform their body parts into weapons with their will power. When young Tomoo with his hand-turned-pistol kills his father, who accidentally murders his wife playing an S/M game during intercourse, the father's experiment on his own sons backfires. The primal scene bloodbath, Tomoo's painful rites of passage, implies that the mutation of the human body into cyborgs is self-destructive. Tomoo from then on suffers amnesia, repressing the traumatic past till he reunites with his brother, Yazu, and his iron-man gang.

Seeking shelter in the selective memory of his childhood, Tomoo tries to resist the violence inherent in his body. His amnesia about the loss of his birth parents makes the happy scene of walking with his family in an idyllic open space of Tokyo a comfort in the everyday life surrounded by the cold, inhuman high-rises presented through harsh blue filtered shots. The buildings are seen through his eyes, which become the eyes of the audience. Tomoo tells Kana about this recurrent dream: "I was in an open space with my family. I was a child again.... It was a wonderful dream. Very peaceful." In the self-deluding memory, all traces of violence are erased. Memory convinces Tomoo that he is anything but a metal fetishist like his father or brother. In other words, Tomoo as a salaryman represents the power of mimesis to deny his lineage of the Iron Man tribe. As required by the civil society, the boy has to forget the incident of patricide. He later grows up with his foster parents and becomes a model salaryman in Tokyo instead of following, like his brother, the path paved by their father and becomes the leader of the underground gang. Through repression and mimesis, Tomoo's real self as a cyborg is tamed and contained temporarily by his docile salaryman identity.

For all his efforts, Tomoo's resistance to the Iron Man identity fails due to the assaults of the cyborgs. Every time one of his family members is abducted, we see how powerless the salaryman's resistance is vis-à-vis the metal-flesh tribe. For example, in the second abduction of his son, Tomoo runs after the kidnapper as fast as he can through the stairs to the top of the building. The breathless father's hurried footsteps along with his panic expression are followed by the shots of the salaryman driven to the edge of the building and his struggle to climb back in the building. Tomoo can hardly protect himself from the strong iron-man thugs, not to mention rescue his family. The shots of the cold steel-and-iron structure of the building in which they fight and the numerous surrounding high-rises further highlight the vulnerability of the salaryman's human body. Ultimately, the repressed returns in a more powerful way than Tomoo can imagine. Tomoo's extreme rage at the attacker who gestures to drop his son to the ground from the high-rise turns his hand into a pistol, which fires at the kidnapper but kills the son by mistake. Devastated, Tomoo is later kidnapped and forced to undergo an experiment of meshing his body with steel in the underground skinhead faction. Mini-cannons exude from his chest and his back whenever the gentle salaryman is overwhelmed by fury. The failure of resistance, so inevitable given the flesh versus steel contrast, seems to imply the frailty and even a delusional attribute of both the utopian memory of an idyllic past that constantly flashes back in Tomoo's dreams and the happy family life in the present.

Confronted with the mounting pressures from the cyborg-gang, Tomoo ultimately makes a final decision to stay alive: giving up the resistance to being a cyborg and turning himself again into a weapon-loaded metal lump. That is, Tomoo chooses to be assimilated into the cyborg gang and mimics the violence of his environment. Shooting a cannon from his arm, Tomoo finds the destructive power of his iron man identity fascinating. The salaryman has come to a point that his mutation into a walking arsenal becomes the only way to deal with his repressed past and the imminent danger facing him. No longer resisting the iron-man gene in his body, Tomoo accepts his transformed body, which endows him with a power that he has never known. Tomoo furthers his own metamorphosis by stretching out his metal tentacles to the foreheads of all the iron men in the tribe and sucking the whole tribe into his body. Tomoo goes through the ordeal of becoming metal himself to avoid the seemingly inevitable fate of being a victim of the iron-man tribe and the similarly hostile buildings of Tokyo. The salaryman's transformation is indeed a result of being seduced by the steel city. At the end of his transformation, Tomoo becomes a grotesque tank loaded with metal mass.

The film bespeaks of an eerie tale of mimicry: to hold on to the idyllic dream or to survive at all, Tokyoites have to act as if they were dead so as to be identical with the fleshless ruins. With his iron-man body, Tomoo destroys the villains, including the underground cyborgs that disrupt his happy family life, and the sinister buildings that shatter his dream of walking in an open space. Ironically, the shattered dream resurfaces after his mimicry of the environment. Looking at the shattered skyscrapers at a distance, Tomoo's wife says contentedly: "It's so peaceful." What we see is a happy picture of the salaryman regaining his human body and getting together with his family to enjoy a leisured walk in an idyllic open space like he used to do as a kid. It is through mimicking the steel-and-concrete space that Tomoo survives the violence and realizes the idyllic dream.

Of a Man and a Building: *Tokyo Fist*

While the salaryman-heroes undergo self-mutilation to integrate their bodies with cybernetic heavy metal in the *Tetsuo* series, the mild-mannered salaryman protagonist in *Tokyo Fist* endeavors to transform himself with blood, perspiration, and pain in the boxing gym. Specifically, the film is about Tokyo's urban space *per se* as perceived by director Tsukamoto, a native Tokyoite growing up witnessing the urbanization of Tokyo from the 1960s to the construction boom of the 1980s. Tsukamoto has been explicit about the theme of urban space in this film in one of his interviews:

> I was born and grew up in Tokyo, so I grew up with those buildings. I was small, and buildings were small at first. Then the buildings became bigger as I grew up. That strange intimacy with the buildings and the city is analogous to the mixed feelings for the parents: affections and fears are two sides of the same coin.

Fascinated by such ambivalent feelings toward Tokyo, Tsukamoto produces *Tokyo Fist* to play out the possibilities of living in a city that tends to be more and more dominated by the steel-and-concrete built environment and the high-tech virtual space. Tsukamoto's drama of a love triangle among Tsuda, an unassuming Tokyo salaryman, his live-in girlfriend and a semi-professional boxer turns out to be something close to a thrilling urban folklore of space, or of the interactions between the human body and the city in the age of globalization.

I intend to explain the paradoxes of life in Tokyo by tracing the protagonist's change from a model salaryman-walker to a disoriented roamer in the city as triggered by his reunion with the boxer Kojima and his confrontation of his repressed memory of a highway murder. I will first discuss the average salaryman's life as a critique of the elevated subjectivity defined by mimesis. Following Tsuda's routine walk, we see the restructured cityscape after the construction boom. The clusters of buildings that make Tokyo into Lefebvre's abstract space *par excellence* stage their presence everywhere in the salaryman's urban life. Tsukamoto's filmic images visualize the duplicity of Tokyo's high-rises: the dazzling buildings of Tokyo seem to dwarf, compress, and hollow out the body of the inhabitants more than honoring them as members of a prosperous and powerful global metropolis.

Like the two salaryman-protagonists in the *Tetsuo* series, Tsuda leads a routine life in Tokyo. As a hard-working insurance salesman, he will be settling down with his office-lady girlfriend Hizuru and be ready for a pension plan long before the age of retirement. Yet a chance encounter with his old friend Kojima significantly changes how Tsuda interacts with the city. Rather than a safe and reliable living space for the salaryman's years to come, the city becomes a boxing ring where one has to fight to survive. Running into Kojima on the street many years after their high-school days, Tsuda soon finds out that Kojima intends to seduce his girlfriend, who, intrigued by Kojima's world of violence and masculinity, breaks up with Tsuda and moves into Kojima's shabby wooden house. Infuriated by losing his woman to Kojima, Tsuda begins a grueling boxing gym routine in the hope of training himself to be a ferocious fighter for revenge. Unfortunately, the salaryman's angry fist neither wins the beauty back nor defeats his rival.

To some extent, Tsuda's story demonstrates the paradoxes of life in Tokyo. What the eye sees all the time (the feel-good-monumental buildings) fails to answer what the body experiences (powerlessness). The inhabitant is defined as the proud user of the new cityscape yet is unable to keep up with the fast-changing space, feeling compressed by the shrinking urban space yet unable to articulate what is wrong. Fascinated and exhausted by the dazzling global city, walkers in Tokyo like Tsuda experience what can be called a "split personalities" syndrome, torn between the abstracted body and the aggrandized subjectivity as a norm both produced by the logic of abstract space.

Walking as a Salaryman: What's Wrong With it?

The representation of Tsuda's life as a normal salaryman walking everyday in the city exemplifies the power of mimesis. The ideal rational relationship between the body and the city is illustrated by where and how Tsuda walks in the city. For one thing, Tsuda's efficient and zesty walking in Tokyo indicates the salaryman's devotion to his job, a proper social relation in the interest of the circuit of capital in the abstract space. Commuting from a high-rise apartment building to work in another high-rise office building in Tokyo, Tsuda walks in the city all day long making door-to-door sales. From the subway station to his office building, from corporate buildings to apartment complexes, Tsuda's daily routine is all about such type of goal-oriented walking. The camera shows Tsuda's walking with his body in various relations to the buildings around him. The proximity between the walker and the buildings implies the function of mimesis, which imposes a symbiotic harmony between the pedestrians and where they walk. Every morning the smooth pedestrian flow formed by thousands of dark-suited, diligent salarymen like Tsuda, makes the giant city-machine operate efficiently. At the same time, the salaryman depends on the city not only for his livelihood but also for his sense of identity, which can be summarized as "I walk/work, and therefore I am."[5]

The shots of the successful reproduction of social relations as shown by the protagonist's walking simultaneously reveal the repressive nature of the global city. Following Tsuda's sales-calls, the camera zooms in on the façade of an anonymous apartment building. Like Tsuda, we see nothing but the building. The camera then zooms out to show the barely visible Tsuda climbing the stairs. While Tsuda is the focus of the *mise-en-scene*, we see a tiny little body with only the head and part of the shoulder in the shot. As Tsuda takes more stairs, his body is engulfed by the space of the building. A close-up of the sweating salaryman cuts to the building's façade again, a symmetrical honeycomb for Tsuda to walk through. Soon enough Tsuda is the same dwarf walking in another gigantic beehive-looking building maze. In fact, every shot of Tsuda's walking for his sales calls conveys a sense of claustrophobia and loneliness. Despite his diligent footsteps, all he encounters is indifferent customers and compressing buildings. Interestingly, if we eliminate the walker in the shots, the images of the buildings in fact very much resemble the conceived space as it appeared in the drafts of the architects and urban planners. These shots of the buildings, as a perfectly designed geometrical space, and the stunted human body contained in the fragmentary box within boxes, are some of the most expressive images throughout the film, suggesting the subjugation of the body by the repressive abstract space of Tokyo.

Tsuda's walking experience, as being hollowed out by the rational, geometrical space, is summarized by the last shot of the sequence of Tsuda's walking as a salesman. Standing exhaustedly in front of big apartment buildings, the sweating salaryman looks up to see a tiny strip of blue sky diced up by the skyscrapers. The buildings around him seem to expand infinitely in all directions. One cannot tell if these are the ones Tsuda just visited or those he will visit next. Like the silent strangers in their separate cubes in the apartment buildings, the high-rises offer Tsuda no return look. The salaryman's one-way gaze seems to be the last link between the body and the building. The weary walker looking anxiously at the buildings points to the sensory experiences of walking in the city, the pressure and weariness that can be repressed but not eradicated.

The images of both Tsuda's family life as well as his home located in the beehive apartment building accentuate the abstraction of Tsuda's body experience as a result of conforming to the demands of the city life. Similar to the clients in the buildings he visits in the daytime, Tsuda and Hizuru correspond to Lefebvre's example of those tenants of stacked up apartment buildings, rewarded by the illusory "whole" at the cost of their lived space (98). The recurring shot of Tsuda dozing on his girlfriend Hizuru's shoulder in front of the TV illustrates the "quality" of their quality time. Like the workers exploited first by the repetition at the workplace and then by the repetition of cultural industry as Theodor Adorno describes, Tsuda marks his time at home by the TV program schedule. Drained of his energy by walking throughout the city, Tsuda doesn't have much stamina left for his after hours. When Hizuru inquires if he is working too hard, Tsuda comforts his girlfriend that "everything is fine at my work." Yet later Tsuda confesses that he has a physical checkup to find out what makes him exhausted. For all his efforts to rationalize the unreasonably demanding city life, overworked Tsuda is overwhelmed by fatigue, a symptom of a body drained by the duties of a model citizen.

Presenting Tsuda as such a normal man in Tokyo, the director poses the question of the cost of normalization with the recurrent and involuntary flashback of a murder scene that Tsuda witnessed in his adolescence under the Tokyo Metropolitan Expressway. This memory is a defining event for both Tsuda and Kojima. Deeply repressed by Tsuda, the murder is revealed instead by Kojima. Recounting the secret bond between these two old friends to Hizuru, Kojima explains that he cannot wait to see Tsuda's face crushed since Tsuda's face reminds him of the girl killed by a gang of reckless teenage boys. The replay of the memory suggests an attempted gang rape which ends with the girl in school uniform being killed by a big knife stuck in her chest. Kojima sees how she dies but cannot fight back against the gang. One step late, Tsuda only makes it to see the girl he admires dead with her eyes wide-opened in an abandoned corner of the city. Tsuda and Kojima are angry and obsessed with finding out who killed the girl. Unfortunately, they are late again for their revenge plan: before they can take any action, the police find the murderers and put them in jail. The juridical justice seems to close the case but the consequences of the homicide continue to be played out in Tsuda's and Kojima's life. Now the only way for these two teenagers to vent their anger and frustration is to come to the crime scene, get drunk, pound on the beams, and pour red paint on themselves.[6] Swearing to train themselves to be killing machines so as to avenge the girl after the murderers do their time, Kojima keeps his word and becomes a professional boxer, but after high school Tsuda seems to forget the whole thing and becomes a salaryman, a "nobody" in Kojima's eyes.

For Tsuda, his normalization is impossible without repressing this traumatic murder event. Contrary to what Kojima believes, Tsuda has never forgotten what happened under the highway. Witnessing the cruelly murdered body of the girl was a rite of passage for Tsuda, which determines his future relation to the urban space. It is not that Tsuda leaves the past behind. The truth is that he is left to drag his footsteps along what abstract space prescribes for him ever since he is overwhelmed by the violence as experienced under the Expressway. Conditioned to give up the irrational idea of deviating from the norm, Tsuda becomes a good young man in "My Town Tokyo." Simply put, Tsuda is the product of abstract space, which suppresses any violence that might endanger the reproduction of role models in the city. The unrealized pledge thus marks the violence of mimesis, a process of containing and constraining a not-yet-indoctrinated body. On a symbolic level, what happens in the abandoned space of the city one full moon night during Tsuda's teenage years seals his fate as a helpless salaryman always outpaced and overpowered by the urban space. In a sense, the gangsters who stab the girl to death are allegorical culprits of the crime, the accomplice of the dark corner of the city under the gigantic columns of the highway. They are only the human agents that enact the violence of the space on the body.

What haunts Tsuda all these years is not the faces of the murderers but the blood-stained hidden corner of Tokyo where he saw her penetrated body and his own despair. Guilty, angry, and frustrated, Tsuda has been tortured by the memory since the very night she was murdered. As the narrative unfolds, the girl's dead body under the Expressway proves to be Tsuda's repressed vision that returns in the forms of the dead cat in a narrow alley between buildings, Tsuda's dying father in the hospital, and Hizuru with her body pierced at every orifice. Seen in this light, the girl is not the only victim of the crime: when she is pierced by the phallic knife and symbolically gang raped, Tsuda's and Kojima's adolescent sexual desire is frustrated. The teenage ego aspiring to be a superman drives Kojima to hold on to the plan of revenge made in his liminal stage of life, whereas Tsuda falls behind the adolescent ambition and becomes more and more subjugated by the social space of the city. Tsuda assumes that emulating the model of the salaryman works as an antidote to the violence hidden in obscure corners of the city, yet ironically, as the plot unfolds, the defense strategies for survival turn out to be giving up the salaryman's identity and mimicking the violence he witnesses.

The major setting of the story is the realistic landscape of Tokyo. The crime scene, the Tokyo Metropolitan Expressway, is not an incidental choice. The repressed memory of Tsuda also points to an often forgotten chapter of Tokyo in its current form of glistening skyscrapers. According to Noriyuki Tajima, originally built to connect the scattered stadiums for the 1964 Tokyo Olympics, more than a decade before the construction boom triggered by globalization, the Expressway marks the entry of Tokyo into the array of global cities. This massive monumental structure later expands through all of Tokyo, the highway stretching as far as Tokyo's hinterland such as Chiba and Yokohama. With its 30 sections over 220 kilometers in length and huge supporting beams, the gigantic highway dominates the cityscape, dwarfs many buildings by contrast, and weaves its way to Tokyoites' doorsteps. Connected with other transportation networks such as railways, subways, bullet trains and pedestrian bridges, the Tokyo Metropolitan Expressway is almost ubiquitous in Tokyoites' daily life (17). With his adolescent memory locked under a dark spot of the Tokyo Metropolitan Expressway, what the salaryman

Tsuda now sees is the compacted high-rise buildings including Shinjuku's skyscrapers, the New City Hall, and suburban housing projects. For Tsuda, the growing-up experiences are parallel to the history of Tokyo becoming a global city. It is also arguable that Tsuda's relationship with the fast changing Tokyo is a sort of projection of the director's own growing-up experiences in Tokyo.

The unexpected reappearance of Kojima, the other witness to the murder under the highway, serves as a catalyst to crack open Tsuda's tightly sealed memory. The director Tsukamoto is persistently concerned with the theme of pressures from the urban space. Again, like Yazu, the leader-brother of the salaryman Tomoo in *Tetsuo II: Body Hammer*, Kojima is the "twin" of Tsuda, the possibility of becoming an "iron-man," who refuses to be codified by social normalization. The truth is that Kojima, Tsuda's model of masculine power, is only deceptively an antithesis of the wimpy Tsuda. For all his impressive muscles and different life style, Kojima is as much subdued by the abstract space of Tokyo as Tsuda. At first glance, Kojima slips away from the normalizing corporate culture and the standard path of a salaryman life, the social/spatial relations in rhyme with the demands of the global city. Noticeably, the old house Kojima rents is within walking distance to Tsuda's modern apartment building. As Kojima says to Tsuda, "We are so close except the life style." The shots of Kojima's humble abode contrasts not only Tsuda's living unit in the high-rise, but the gigantic buildings right behind it: a mirror image of the juxtaposition of Ohkawabashi River City 21 and the local housing of Tsukuda-jima. In contrast to Tsuda's highly fragmented living space in the apartment building, Kojima's traditional Japanese wooden house reminds us of a past less dominated by the abstract space of the global city. Like the cheap wooden house he inhabits, Kojima seems to demonstrate the untamed body that refuses to be abstracted by the abstract space of globalization.

Kojima might not be boxed within the claustrophobic Bauhausian high-rise like Tsuda, yet the boxer's spatial and social practices are no less dictated by the power of the global city. In a sense, Kojima's life style, instead of serving as an ideal alternative to a good salaryman like Tsuda, divulges the horror of walking in the city without the salaryman's bearings, the consequence of not modeling after an ideal type of citizen. Professionally, Kojima is by no means a first-rate boxer. His shabby house is slum-like, reflecting a career without life-long employment guarantee and seniority promotion, a job that often requires early retirement after the prime time of the body or severe damage in the next game. Indeed, Kojima has never been immune from the violence of the space of decorporealization. Two shots illustrate vividly that Kojima's lived space is manipulated by the capitalist space of the city. A shot of Kojima staring at the electric transmission of paper boxes in front of him suggests his moonlighting as a mover is no less monotonous and exploitative than that of a salaryman. A follow-up shot with deep focus cinematography shows Kojima being surrounded by anonymous buildings while reading carefully the newspaper classifieds in the hope of finding some odd jobs. The electric wire spreading above him among the buildings resembles a spider web waiting for the prey.

Both *Tetsuo II: Body Hammer* and *Tokyo Fist* allegorize the oppression of the space through the main character's pain of losing his beloved. In parallel to Yazu's kidnapping of Tomoo's family members, Kojima seduces Tsuda's girlfriend away from him. The prospect of losing Hizuru to Kojima opens a Pandora's box for Tsuda. The memory of the dead teenager comes back to haunt him. In this sense, Kojima is a trickster of the urban space, who forces Tsuda to open his eyes to the morbid ruins repressed under the surface of the glittering city.

Tokyo Fist is certainly not limited to a lover's quarrel; rather, the director dramatizes an existential questioning of the urban space in general. Tsuda finds it harder to cling to his salaryman identity in the city when his father passes away in the hospital. While in the background the nurse says "[y]our father died in peace without pain," shoved in the audience's face is the façade of the buildings through the blinds of the hospital ward, providing a clear image of the strangers on the street rather than Tsuda's response. He has been prepared for his father's death for a long time, but still was unable to make it to the deathbed in time. The empty bed suggests that once again Tsuda is one step too late for the scene. Falling behind results in irresolvable melancholia for Tsuda, and the supposedly paternal city only intensifies Tsuda's unspeakable sense of loss with its hollow concrete and crowds. In short, Tsuda's personal loss is trivialized by the overpowering landscape of Tokyo. The speedy sequence of building shots ends with a panoramic view of the skyscrapers of Shinjuku. The following shot of the continuous flows of walkers in the street not only sharply contrasts the sudden disruption of Tsuda's life but also signifies an indifferent crowd in sync with the compassionless city. No longer looking for a return gaze from the crowds or a sense of familiarity in the buildings, Tsuda the salaryman finds "My Town Tokyo" disappearing everywhere he goes.

Disheartened, Tsuda is defeated once again by the space when Hizuru fails to show up under the highway as promised. Tsuda finds himself drawn back to the crime scene, where he waits for Hizuru as his last resource to seek consolation. The meeting place is by no means randomly chosen. In a sense, psychologically Tsuda never leaves the space under the Expressway after the night of the homicide. As dividers and enclosures of Tokyo's cityscape (Tajima 18), the highway plays a similar role on a symbolic level in Tsuda's life. It marks the dividing line between Tsuda's adolescent aspiration and his later average salaryman days, between a world of brutal violence and a safe haven of order, which are paradoxically the same urban space. Lurking somewhere in his unconscious, the violence he experiences at the dark space of the city's monumental structure has become part of him. Provoked first by Kojima's trick and then his father's death, Tsuda walks back to the starting point where he becomes overwhelmed by the violence in the space and subsequently conditioned by the violence of the space to emulate the model of the honorable salaryman. Like the previous shots of the geometrically perfect buildings, the Expressway is presented as a conceived space that compresses the body. The vacant spot created by the Expressway where Tsuda keeps coming back physically and emotionally after being tricked by Kojima is only deceptively an open space for Tsuda to free his repressed feelings. Structurally, the highway and its supporting beams have always enclosed it; psychologically, Tsuda seeks liberation of his feelings here since he is tied up by this space in the first place.

Standing under the highway, Tsuda looks small and vulnerable in contrast to the symmetrical giant pillars. When Tsuda comes back to the space under the highway as a private space of letting go of his emotions many years after the murder, he finally faces what has been suppressed by his salaryman life in the city, the sexual and the sensual. The serpentine-like Expressway that traverses the city twists around Tsuda's body and almost conveys a mythical sense, echoing the python sent by Poseidon to strangle the prophet Laocoön in the *Iliad*. Laocoön is killed for his knowledge of the Trojans' scheme, yet what secret knowledge does Tsuda hold if not the violence of the space? Thus seen, Tsuda's revisiting the crime scene is not a conscious attempt to exorcise the demon in him by confronting the space itself but an unwitting seduction by the power of the space the way a moth is attracted to flames. The high-school love is lost to the abject space of the city forever and many years later at the same place Tsuda confirms that he has lost another girl.

The urban space of Tokyo proves to be overwhelming and disorienting. With the loss of his father and his girlfriend, Tsuda abandons himself into a ghost-like drifting in Tokyo; he is swallowed up by the space, so to speak. From the marvelous New City Hall complex to anonymous buildings, from the subway station to the fire lane between high-rises, from the Expressway to the sewers, Tsuda wanders from one place to another. Looking at the high-rises, the walker only sees a city with miles of buildings with no return gaze. The salaryman walks to the subway station without knowing where to go and what to do. Tsuda stands in a rather empty subway train car and stares straight expressionlessly as if he were not there. The following expressionist image shows Tsuda standing in the subway station with glass windows shining behind the dark figure of his body. The montage of a moving train superimposed on a motionless Tsuda creates the effect of the train passing through Tsuda's evacuated body; further hints at the decorporealizing forces of the city as represented by the daily commuting. An ensuing shot of Tsuda gazing at the pedestrian flows also indicates the malfunction of mimesis. The way Tsuda looks at the crowd walking out of the subway escalator is presented as if he were looking among them for a lost self from the previous life. The walker's gaze is supposed to anchor his salaryman identity and maintain the ideal relationship with the space, but now Tsuda can neither see in the buildings around him the sublime and the monumental nor find a model to emulate among the pedestrian crowds.

In such a disorienting whirlpool of Tokyo, Tsuda cannot find any reference point except the overwhelming space itself. When disavowing the violence of the city so as to live as an ideal salaryman seems to be an inadequate survival strategy, Tsuda responds to the suffocating urban space by mimicking the violence of the metropolis. Finally getting to see Hizuru under the Expressway on her way back to cook dinner for Kojima, the only thing the hollow man Tsuda can do now is to abuse himself and Hizuru. He imitates and displaces the violence inflicted on him from the external surrounding onto Hizuru and his own body. The pain of constantly being overwhelmed by a sense of insignificance, helplessness, belatedness now turns to a relentless physical torment of self and others. Ironically, when Tsuda finally gets to confront what really takes Hizuru away, the power of violence inherent in the space, Hizuru has been completely seduced by Kojima the sorcerer and is obsessed with various ways of imposing violence on the body, particularly un-anesthetized body piercing. As the always-belated Tsuda keeps hitting his head against the wall, Hizuru with a radish in her left hand hits him harder with several right hooks, telling the bloody Tsuda that "you can't beat it."[7] Hizuru is then punched to the ground as she tells Tsuda that she doesn't mind Kojima beating her to death. What follows is a repetition of the maniac-fighting scenario: Tsuda cannot stop hitting his head against the pillars of the Expressway and hitting Hizuru, who punches him in return like a professional boxer. When it turns dark, Tsuda's bloody face is hardly intelligible, and Hizuru's bruised and swollen. Several bouts of fights later Hizuru leaves with her now split in half radish, and Tsuda with his beaten up body alone under the highway. The lovebirds' reunion now only simulates the sad encounters between the pathetic mimic insects Phyllias, which prey on each other because they cannot tell the foliage from another Phyllia. Noticeably, the final shot of Tsuda standing in the middle of a busy street trying to raise his arms fades out with an impressive bird's-eye view of Tokyo's skyscrapers, followed by a sequence of cityscape shots. The bright lights and shining façade of the buildings, the traffic flowing on the Expressway, and the fast-moving trains contrast the dysfunctional salaryman with a lost soul and a beaten-up body.

Tsuda's delight in cruelty is not so much a defiance against the violence of the space as it is a survival instinct developed as he experiences the imminent danger of his existence but is unable to identify the predators beyond the loser-boxer Kojima and the unfaithful Hizuru. Like the fight with Hizuru, the sadomasochistic violence entailed in Tsuda's final confrontation with Kojima in the boxing ring typifies the mechanism of mimicry. Every round of their fight is intertwined with the shots of the various angles of the skyscrapers, the built environment of capitalist space. The silent buildings not so much contrast the animalistic fighters as suggest another invincible opponent. The gory montage of Kojima's bruised face imposed on the city streets, buildings, and pedestrians further testifies to the parallel roles of Kojima and Tokyo, envisioned by the crushed Tsuda with blood gushing out from every orifice.

The survival instinct seen in the phenomenon of mimicry thus offers potential insights into the sadomasochistic nature of urban violence demonstrated in Tsuda's painful social relationships. When physical pain induced from the compressed lived space becomes the only signifier of an invisible power, the subject plays with pain to assume the power of the environment and in so doing survives the violence inflicted by the space. In other words, the only way to avert being devoured by the dark space is to be the dark space itself. Performance thus becomes the ultimate disguise to redeem the subject from being destroyed as a victim by abstract space. He or she can choose to play the role of the master, an agent of power that inflicts physical pain on others (sadism). Or, the subject can choose to stage his or her own suffering, playing the part of a victim rather than simply being a victim (masochism). Assuming power and taking control of his or her own suffering, the masochist differentiates him or herself from the passive recipient of pain (Noyes 157). In the game of "S & M," bodily pain becomes an imaginary source of power. The more intense the pain is, the more pleasure the sadomasochist gains: the sweetness of power lies in the excruciating physical torment. The masochist therefore constantly re-enacts the suffering of the body to assure him or herself the accessibility of power. In short, while mimesis defines the proper spatial and social relations for the occupant of abstract space, mimicry shows the repressed body evolving to replicate what it experiences during the subject-formation process.

The last shot of Tsuda in his dark salaryman suit looking at the crowd walking on the street, identical to the establishing shot we saw of him as the film began, frames the narrative and hints at the dual nature of abstract space and its inherent violence. Critically injured in his duet with Kojima, Tsuda is hospitalized and bandaged like a mummy. The camera moves from the blood gushing out from Tsuda's bandage-covered face and the empty bed in the ward to the busy traffic and millions of commuters walking on the streets, then finally to Tsuda going back to his commuting routine. As we see at the beginning of the film, Tsuda stands on an elevated pedestrian passage in his salaryman attire apparently coming out of a station. With half of his face in dark shadow, Tsuda stares at the crowds walking down on the streets with a blank look as the train passes by behind him. The director seems to suggest at the end of the film, by using the same shot, that the salaryman ultimately retrieves his normal life after the violence is over. Tsuda appears to be ready to join the pedestrian flows and resume his usual life after a wild episode in which he releases his repressed physical energies. Yet a closer look at the image of the salaryman's body reveals that the frame shots of Tsuda as a salaryman re-affirm the pathogenic nature of the space. Skillfully overlapping with the unhealed wounds from the fight, the strange shadow on the protagonist's face makes Tsuda look ghostly in the broad daylight. The surreal image of Tsuda illuminates the condition of living in a city subject to global capital: walking in abstract space as a salaryman, Tsuda is not too different from an apparition.[8] The ocean of blood that saturates the story of a salaryman's walking in Tokyo indeed allegorizes the decorporealizing violence of abstract space.

The absurdity of Tsuda's life lies in his blindness to what he really grapples with: the power that reduces him to a clown or puppet has never shown its face. Hizuru's sarcastic comments on Kojima seem to be more apt for the salaryman's life in Tokyo: "You think you are a boxer. But you ain't. Instead, you are a clown, swinging up and down in the ring like a monkey. Everyone knows that but you. A big joke who doesn't know how to fight." No one knows how to fight since what inflicts the pain, the abstract space of Tokyo, is everywhere but also paradoxically invisible. Tsuda has been trying to avenge Kojima for shattering his normal life. Nevertheless, the normal life that Tsuda thinks he is fighting for is ironically what he really fights against, the imprisoning routine life rendering him to serve abstract space. The violence he takes on is the violence of the very space he inhabits. Like the stick insects (phasmids) that derive their names from the Latin word phasma meaning phantom, Tsuda in the mirroring shots that frame the film is phantom-like. If a stick insect's living condition can be boiled down to "resembling a twig but not a twig," the crux of salaryman Tsuda's life in the global city is "simulating an abstract space but not an abstract space," an on-going dialectic between mimesis and mimicry, between the global flows and the carnal flows.

PART THREE

Mirror, Mirror, On the Wall:
Walking in Shanghai, A Global City in the Making

> Under the conditions of modernity, as absolute political space extends its sway, the impression of transparency becomes stronger and stronger, and the illusion of a new life is everywhere reinforced. Real life indeed appears quite close to us. We feel able, from within everyday life, to reach out and grasp it, as though nothing lay between us and the marvellous reality on the other side of the mirror.
>
> Henri Lefebvre

> In a nutshell, Shanghai is not sensual any more. New buildings construct a new cover for it, which separates the city from the physical senses of its inhabitants. Such a fancy cover, however, does not fit perfectly. There is always some empty space in between the exterior and the real thing. Or maybe it is due to the fact that we are too close to the city and it happens to undergo drastic changes. All the visions are blurred.
>
> Wang Anyi

Rome was not built in a day: Western megalopolises like New York, London, or Paris all seem to testify to the validity of the saying. However, contemporary East Asian metropolises often prove otherwise. Tokyo, as described in Part Two, was rebuilt into a global city within three decades (roughly from the late 1960s to the early 1990s). A more stunning example is Shanghai. Upon seeing Shanghai's formation into a global showcase[1] with the mobilization of capital globalization since the late 1970s with China's open door policy, whoever thinks that Rome was not built in a day would definitely think twice.[2] Reaching its peak in the 1990s, the massive urban construction Manhattanizes Shanghai with an impressive new skyline and high-rises everywhere in the city. If in doubt, a mere look at the luminous cluster of skyscrapers of Pudong's Lujiazui and all the commercial signs of world-famous corporations might assure the skeptics.

Ever since the launching of the Pudong New Area development in 1990 on the east bank of the Huangpu River, Pudong has become the most pronounced articulation of the urban planning of Shanghai. Born at the end of the twentieth century with the prevalent image of "first-class world cities" as unanimously acclaimed city of the future, Pudong is conceived as a global city like New York, London, Tokyo, or Hong Kong. No one can overlook the fact that with the reformation of Pudong, "the golden highway between China and the world" in the vice-mayor's words (Streshinsky 38), Shanghai is a global city in the making. Ironically, the fancy new look demonstrated by Pudong conceals the fact that the polarized other, the banal lived space of everyday life is compressed by the large-scale urban redevelopment. One distinctive characteristic of global city formation is that on the one hand the capitalist-friendly urban space often demands local inhabitants should be amenable to urban changes in the face of new circumstances. As the famous slogan for Shanghai's urban development goes: "Development is the irrefutable truth (發展是硬道理)." At the same time, the global city invites the inhabitants to identify themselves as city-users, to claim the new city as their own without suspecting that the current urban space might not be as accessible as they are convinced.[3]

Part Three aims to explore how Shanghai's urban restructuring, predominantly modeled on the image of a generic global city, informs us of the problematics of globalization which subsumes the concrete space of people's daily life under the logic of capital accumulation. My central argument is that Shanghai can be seen as built in the dual images of a mirror within a mirror. On a macro-global level, existing global cities in the world present themselves as role models for Shanghai's urban renewal plans. Concomitantly, on the micro-personal level, Old Shanghai before globalization becomes another mirror image on which individuals can anchor an image of the new Shanghai with a particular emphasis on urban culture and daily life.

Continuing to use the montage methodology in Parts One and Two, I will superimpose a social account of Shanghai's urban development since the Pudong Special Zone was conceived and constructed as a global financial center with an artistic representation of contemporary Shanghai in novelist Wang Anyi's works. The discussion will focus on not only the production of the space, the material development of Pudong and Shanghai, which simultaneously projects an ideal image of the city for users to identify with, but also the social conflicts engendered by such conceived space of the global city. The juxtaposition of the discourse/implementation of Shanghai's urban development and the fictional representation of the city opens a window through which one can see the effects of Shanghai's globalization on its inhabitants. To be precise, the global city Shanghai, as demonstrated by Pudong, is more of a monumental space, a capitalist showcase rather than the lived space the novelist would call home. To be able to claim the new urban space as her own, Wang Anyi needs to compose an alternative image that addresses the concrete space of daily life in the hope of completing the prevalent rational space of capitalism. Thus, the mirror of Pudong and the mushrooming high-rises in the city easily turns her to another mirror, the Old Shanghai alley houses harboring nuances of everyday life and memories. I argue that Wang's representation of Shanghai, a persistent project of anthropologically dissecting every detail of *lilong*[4] life rather than the postcard image of Shanghai's trendy space, foregrounds the lived space, what has been overshadowed (suppressed) as a consequence of the development of the global city. Yet, the author's zealous efforts to define an authentic Shanghai by filling in "the void" produced by the capitalist space with myriad images of the past ironically corroborates the power of the abstract space of the global city. When the capitalist space is envisioned as transparent and malleable, an empty container ready for the user to fill out, the problemtics inherent in such a space threatens to go unchallenged fundamentally.

In the fictional narratives under discussion, walking, the seemingly outdated pedestrian act against the background of fast-paced global city, serves as a metaphor for remembering the past or a practice of everyday life, as well as a political unconscious for the author to articulate the otherwise unrepresentable conflicts between the new Shanghai as an emerging global metropolis and the concrete space called home.

6

"Build It and They Will Come":
Transformation of Pudong into
a Copy of the Global City

April 18, 1990, should definitely be marked as one of the significant dates in the urban history of Shanghai. When the then Premier, Li Peng, announced that the development of Pudong was the decision of the Party Central Committee and the State Council, Pudong was destined to become the political endorsement of the reforming and opening policy, the symbolic vision of China's future role in the global economy, and the material site for accumulating capital.[1] What had been conceived as a global city before it became one was a low-density residential, agricultural and industrial zone, where one could see "[l]arge areas of wasteland, mid-rise blocks of flats, and old wharves, dockyards and warehouses that stretch along the banks of the Huangpu River" (Lammie 174).[2] A decade later, one witnesses this 350-square-km plot of land, located opposite Shanghai proper across the Huangpu River, being transformed into the latest enclave of multinational corporations, with dazzling skyline and landmark architectures as the new image of Shanghai. President Jiang Zemin's speech at the 1999 Fortune Global Forum in Shanghai speaks for many other government officials' pride in the "Pudong miracle": "Only six years ago, in this Lujiazui District of Shanghai's Pudong area, where we are gathered this evening, there were only run-down houses and farms. Now it is a vibrant modern financial and business zone, full of high-rise buildings." It is noteworthy that the image of the global city is the blueprint for the Pudong new area, or specifically, the Lujiazui Central Area Project: the "ugly duckling" for Jiang Zemin is made over to be another New York, London, or Hong Kong. The operating logic is that for China to join the global club, Shanghai has to market itself as a global city to attract capital flows.[3] The difficulty of making a global financial heartland in the over-packed

Puxi with its labyrinth-like urban space makes Pudong a more convenient choice for the urban planners and developers to materialize their idea of a global city. What is even better for them, here they can build one from scratch.[4] Those who see the space of Pudong as a blank piece of paper ready for the most ambitious spatial expressions cannot wait to plate the "wasteland" with gold overnight.

Pudong: A showcase of global capital.
(Picture taken by the author in January 2001)

Since the day when Pudong was designated the strategic site for China's entry into the global market, the images of global cities have been popular in the urban planning discourse on Pudong's development. For example, in *Shanghai Pudong New Area Handbook*, the master plan is to Manhattanize Pudong: "It [Lujiazui] will be the CBD [central business district] of Pudong, as well as the new CBD of Shanghai. *It is intended to be developed as the Manhattan of Shanghai*" (qtd. in Yeh 279; emphasis mine). Singapore and Hong Kong, two prominent global cities in East Asia, also serve as the success story for Pudong to emulate (Lammie 174).[5] In *Challenging the New Height: The Development of Pudong*, the ethos of building a global city is well illustrated in a comparative chart of "five-star world-cities," including New York, Tokyo,

Hong Kong, Singapore and Pudong, which indicates how Pudong should further develop to erase the differences between its images as a newly rising global city and as a well-recognized world metropolis.[6] The assumption of such a comparison is that Pudong, Shanghai, is now undergoing a "world-city" formation process (Sun and Liu 148–50). By quantifying the concept of a "global city," this specific report on "Renowned World-Cities and the Urbanization of Pudong," calibrated to pin down the otherwise abstract idea of a "world city," provides the planners of Pudong a working chart:

> For Pudong New Area to get as close to[7] other super world-cities as possible so as to achieve its role as the "dragon head". . . . We attempt to present some basic defining qualities of world cities, a set of standards to evaluate world-cities for Pudong and other cities to compare with. (136)[8]

In a sense, the engine that drives Pudong into the future of globalization is the group of "contractor" consultants hired by then-mayor Zhu Rongji to help build Pudong into the city of the twenty-first century after his visit to Europe in 1991. The "French-Chinese Shanghai Lujiazui Central Area International Planning and Urban Design Consultation Committee," funded by the French government, is therefore composed of French official institutions (Olds 1995: 1732). This French Committee manages to get world-famous professional groups from Britain, Italy, Japan, and France to contribute to China's grand plan by having each of them submit its own master plan for Pudong. Pudong becomes the high-profile site for international architects to employ their ideas of high modernity in spatial terms in order to impose an interpretive grid on the city. As Kris Olds describes, the glamorous résumés of these "global intelligence corps" (in P. Rimmer's words) are the living anthology of world architectures: the Centre Pompidou in Paris, the London Docklands, the Sydney Opera House, the Kansai Airport, the HSBC Headquarters, and the list can go on.[9] In short, the project was "pitched to appeal to the architects' desire to inscribe their concepts of urbanity on a postcolonial city being radically transformed into a 21st century international financial center" (Olds 1995: 1732).

In addition to the construction of high-rises, an international airport is indispensable in the plans to maximize Pudong's function as a global financial powerhouse to attract foreign investment. The urgency of building a new airport is ranked the top priority by Sun Haiming and Liu Naichuan in comparing world cities and Pudong:

> As a world city, it is critical to have modern infrastructure. JFK airport in New York, Haneda in Tokyo, Kaitak in Hong Kong, and Singapore's international airport are all capable of taking care of up to 50,000,000 passengers annually, but Pudong doesn't have its own international airport yet. (140)

Since the enactment of the construction plan in 1996, Pudong International Airport with its 280,000-square-meter building space, has been envisioned as the largest airport in Asia. Built in the shape of a seagull at south Pudong, the new airport complements the old Hongqiao airport to cater to the influx of passengers upon its completion in 2000.[10] The airport also plays a vital symbolic role as a statement of the city's ambition for flying into the future. Pudong airport aspires to join the pantheon of Chek Lap Kok Airport of Hong Kong, Narita of Tokyo, and Osaka Kansai International Airport as a sublime object to be identified with.

Undoubtedly, Pudong New Area serves as a locomotive that pushes the urban development of Shanghai into a new stage. The massive-scale construction boom, including both urban infrastructures and buildings for commercial and residential purposes, changes the urban geography remarkably. Pamela Yatsko's observation for *Far Eastern Economic Review* in July 1996 summarizes well what it takes for Shanghai to "reemerge" as a key financial nexus:

> Throughout the city, whole blocks are being flattened, turning parts of the former "Paris of the East" into huge construction sites — a chorus of cranes, jackhammers and bulldozers chiselling out the foundations of skyscrapers, elevated expressways and subway tunnels. Architects are having their fling with modernism — designing huge glass-faced office complexes and luxury apartment blocks. (1996a: 69)

In the words of an official from the city planning authority, this is where Shanghai stands: "64 kilometers (40 miles) of subway and light rail network to be built, 650 kilometers of city highway, *12 million square meters (130 million square feet) of new office space and housing, 265,000 old houses up for demolition, 20 million square meters of existing ones to be renovated*" (Maass 23; emphasis mine). Against the background of construction boom and demolition frenzy, all in the name of making a global city out of Shanghai, the development slogan, "it [the city] will be different every year and radically different every three years (一年一個樣，三年大變樣)," sounds like an understatement.[11]

International capital virtually occupies every inch of metropolitan Shanghai's profitable space, concretized in the steel-and-concrete new high-rises, bridges, and highways, just to name a few examples.

In short, Pudong to a large extent has fulfilled its primary command-and-control function as Shanghai's new CBD, capable of accumulating and deploying international capital.[12] The immense influx of transnational corporations (TNC), as well as the construction boom, indexes Pudong's new role as the nexus of global flows. In 1999, 98 of the global top 500 businesses invested $8.06 billion in 181 projects in the Pudong New Area (Li 13).[13] The fast release of land consequently catalyzes the real-estate boom. One also witnesses an accelerating supply of space in Pudong: "by 1994, virtually all land in Lujiazui's core area had been leased out, which gave 1.69 million square metres of the development space" (qtd. in Wu 1369).[14] According to the Pudong New Area Municipal Administrative Committee, in 1997 alone, 168 over-24-story skyscrapers were under construction, and by 1999, more than 180 high-rises dominated the skyline (Xin 19). Since then, new monumental buildings appear in every picture of contemporary Shanghai circulated in mass media as the latest wonder of the world. Among them, the Orient Pearl Television Tower and the Jinmao Skyscraper of 420 meters, 88 stories of glass and marble, have become the new landmarks of the city. The competition is not over yet: right next to the Jinmao Skyscraper, another high-rise is on its way to the sky. This $750-million project, the new 95-story Global Financial Center, funded by 36 US and Japan financial institutions and the Japan Overseas Foundation, is designed to impress the world as the tallest building on earth upon completion (Maass 23).[15]

Global City Formation: What Can Go Wrong?

When Shanghai is celebrated as another London, New York, Tokyo or Hong Kong, the consequent social conflicts are often downplayed. In the following discussion, I intend to explore the problems entailed by prescribing the global city as the draft for Shanghai's urban restructuring. Specifically, it is not surprising to observe a process of dualization, a tendency which has been evidenced in most global cities in which the newly produced urban space promotes the expansion of the top-level service class and devalues the lived space of the general population.

Saskia Sassen's observation on how the urban geography is increasingly determined by the new user of the city in the age of globalization contributes to a comprehension of Shanghai's urban renewal and its consequences.[16] According to Sassen, one salient feature of the new urban space of global cities is the widening gap between two types of city users, a small group of professionals and a large number of low-income people (1996: 221). For the multinational business people, Sassen asserts, utopia means a city of nice airports, prime-site business districts, and a large variety of leisure establishments (1996: 220).[17] The heart of the problem, as Sassen rightly sees it, is that the claims of the professional managerial class are rarely challenged or questioned, and as a result the urban space of a global city is ceaselessly subjected to the claims imposed by the new users.

The ultramodern office buildings, upscale housing, fancy hotels and trendy restaurants, and the infrastructures like Pudong International Airport and the new highways can all be seen as the forceful articulation of the Shanghai service class's claims to the new urban space, just as what we witnessed in other global cities. Of particular interest here is not so much the ways in which Shanghai qualifies as an ideal city for the TNC elite but rather the fact that what Sassen describes as the international business people's "claims" in the formation of Shanghai's global city campaign are naturalized as prescriptive, conceptual qualifications. In other words, if the space of, for example, Hong Kong, has been constantly redrawn to meet the "needs" of transnational business, in Shanghai the city is constructed in such a way that international business people don't seem to have to lay claim to the urban space, for the claims are already built-in as the prerequisite of the city. The high-profile urban plans submitted by the "global intelligence corps" mean to create instantly a desirable urban image for transnational corporations by disseminating the big names of the architects and their monumental projects (Olds 1995: 1735, Streshinsky 38). Zhu Rongji, famous for his penchant for inviting "foreign monks" as consultants, hires the Consultation Committee for Lujiazui's development plans not so much because of a blind idolization of foreigners but as a marketing strategy to project a credible urban image so as to draw in global capital.[18]

A quick look at the Shanghai municipal government's conceptual plans for Pudong unravels the secret of Shanghai's magical attraction to the service class. In Pudong, "4 million m^2 of space is planned for the main area, including over *2.65 million m^2 of office space, 300000 m^2 of 'luxury housing', and 500000 m^2 of hotel space*" (Olds 1995: 1733; emphasis mine).[19] In 1995, the high-grade office space in the whole of Shanghai was "about 270,000 square metres and is set to grow to 3.24 million square metres within five years. The equivalent area in Hong Kong took about 35 years to build" (Huus 48). Aside from the increasing number of modern office blocks, the upscale housing for foreign expatriate employees also reshapes both Pudong's and Puxi's urban landscape. The concentration of high-priced housing, according to urban geographer Fulong Wu, is one of the leading examples of how globalization has changed Shanghai's urban space. When expensive housing, like the projects clustering in the west part of Shanghai with a price tag from US$150 to 2,650 per square meter, becomes the hot item for the service class, low- and middle-income residents have to be relocated to the peripheral areas of the city (Wu 1364).[20] The local residents have to make room, since the professional managerial class needs not only fancy workplace and housing but also leisure space. For example, those who choose Pudong's luxurious housing assert that "they are increasingly tempted by Pudong's relative merits. . . . A new golf course and roomier housing go a long way . . . " ("Shanghai Takes Shape" 28). Nevertheless, it seems that the real magic of Shanghai for attracting transnational corporations is, after all, the magic of place-making for the purpose of capital accumulation. For the prestigious service class, "a new golf course and roomier housing" might go a long way, but in fact they are essentially poor compensation "for the tiresome aspects of living in a dirty, third-world country" ("Shanghai Takes Shape" 28). When the "claims to the urban space" are implemented for the transnational executives, what is taken for granted is more than the spatial forms catering to their so-called needs.

A byproduct of the process of naturalizing and justifying transnational business people's claims to the urban space is the popular image of "successful people" (成功人士) in the local language. A generic member of "successful people" in commercial films wears brand-name suits, drives a fancy car, patronizes fashionable restaurants and bars, global-trots for business or vacation, and, more importantly, works in one of the ultramodern office buildings and lives in a splendid apartment or villa with servants and maids around. Disseminated by the mass media, such luminous images of successful people seem to "humanize" and concretize for low- and middle-class people the otherwise invisible life led by successful people in such global spaces as the fancy office buildings and the expensive housing.

This emergent social icon illustrates not only the rise of the top-level service class in contemporary Shanghai but also how capitalist space eases the social tension engendered in the dual city by marketing the image of "a well-to-do tomorrow for all." For every Shanghainese to come up with the answer unanimously to the question "Whose city is it," the global space in the possession of the service class has to look accessible for every inhabitant rather than just for the foreigners. The widely circulated representation of so-called "successful people," promulgated by Shanghai's mass media and fashion magazines in the last few years, is exactly a "localized" image of the transnational managerial class, a refraction projected for inhabitants to emulate and thereby further identify with the global space associated with the new rich. The commercial has drilled it into us that if we only have similar taste to that of the successful people (demonstrated by purchasing the commodity), the glittering global space will be at our disposal ("just take a look at these guys"). Wang Xiaoming insightfully points out in his "The Myth of a Half-Revealed Face" that such representation of the new rich is problematic since it is partial in the sense that the image created for us to look up to is incomplete and biased. On the one hand, the public sees only slices of the luxury life of the new elite, as if they did not have any other dimensions of everyday life. More significantly, "the other half of their face," the means to power, money, and social status, always remains unseen (31).

Indeed, one of the effects of the capitalist space of globalization is to make everyone believe that this space is his or her own, regardless of the fact that the city was restructured based on the assumed needs of a small group of multinational service class people, the human agents of global capital. To draw on Wang Xiaoming's interpretation, only when the other face of the iconic city users remains blurred is it possible for the reflections of their image to serve as models: everyone in Shanghai is then likely to see the other half of the face as his or her own (Wang 31). Meanwhile, as Wang argues, the attempt to make the unattainable global space realistic has the paradoxical effect of making the image of the successful people seem very unreal. Such glaring disparities between the intention of the representation and the actual effect interestingly point to the mis-represented distance between the service class and the lower-middle class in everyday life, that is to say, the distance between the monumental space of global capital and the lived space of the local inhabitants.

7

From Alley Houses to High-rises:
What Happened to the Lived Space?

To illuminate how the lived space of ordinary people's everyday life is undermined to serve the expanding space of global flows, I will concentrate on the four most profound impacts on the inhabitants that resulted from Shanghai's global city formation. Above all, to reshape Shanghai into the city of the twenty-first century, migrant workers' claims to the urban space are repressed, numerous local residents relocated, the function of work-units diminished, and thousands of workers in traditional industries laid off.

While the divide between the service class and the majority of the Shanghainese is masked by naturalizing the transnational business people's claims to new urban space as part of the collective desire to see Shanghai rise as a city of the future, the problems of the other end of the duality, the downtrodden laborers, are simply rendered as nonexistent. If the successful people （成功人士）serve as localized reflection and refraction of the international service class, in Shanghai, what corresponds to the foreign laborers as seen in global cities like New York, London, or Hong Kong, is the large number of migrant workers from inland provinces. There has been a long history of Shanghai attracting migrant workers, and the city's recent ongoing urban construction has accounted for another major influx. In 1993 alone, Shanghai mobilized more than 1 million construction workers to complete 18 key urban construction projects (Liao 20). Evidently, most of them are migrant workers, but specifically how many does not seem to be a major concern of the report. One report from the *Economist* estimates that on average about 2 million migrant laborers were looking for jobs in Shanghai every day in 1995 ("City of the Plain" 18). Another study on urban transportation in Shanghai, published in 1997, shows that the "floating population," predominantly rural migrants, is believed to come to 3 million and the number is still growing (Shen 591–2). Yet, the increasing number of the migrant laborers guarantees neither any representation nor any rights. In fact, in the literature on Pudong's or Shanghai's development into a global city, the issue of migrant workers has not been addressed adequately. For instance, in the comparative chart of world-cities and Pudong, no figures of foreign laborers versus migrant workers can be found. When billions of dollars funded by bankers is flowing in, one fifth of the whole world's building cranes are in action, block after block of high-rises are mushrooming at every corner, the question of how many migrant workers are involved with the grand project of building a global city does not seem to matter. What are the counterparts of the fancy office, luxury apartment and verdant golf course of the service class? The slices of the migrant workers' lives in Shanghai — their workplaces, accommodations, and leisure spaces, if any — largely remain unknown. When urban developers are preoccupied with updating the images of transnational corporations in Shanghai, the amount of foreign direct investment, the height of a new monumental building, or even the number of building cranes, those who are physically carrying out the material construction are excluded from the calculated mapping of the global city.

The migrant laborers' claims to the urban space can easily be ignored, since they are non-registered rural people, legally never belonging to Shanghai, due to China's migration policy.[1] Thus they can barely qualify as justifiable users of the city, despite the fact that the physical construction of the shimmering global city relies on their hard labor. In contrast to the image of the successful people, migrant workers are often conflated with such names as "floating population" or "blind drifters," (盲流) the latter with a strong derogatory connotation of chaos and disorder. Their representation, if any, is the undesirable abject that contradicts the collective desire of shaping a clean and proper global city. During my recent visit to Shanghai in January 2001, when inquiring about the migrant workers in Shanghai, I was told that the government aims "to replace 4 million migrant workers (民工) with 4 million professionals." Such a statement provides a striking commentary on the flip side of global city formation, the dual-city vista. In essence, both the service class and the migrant workers are a "floating population," brought into Shanghai by the global flows. Nevertheless, while the service class has a right to the global city even before they lay their claims, the migrant workers are marginalized to such an extent that they are no more human than the building cranes.

The rationally conceived global space as an enclave for the service class is made possible not only by mobilizing Shanghai's millions of migrant workers but also by relocating traditional industries and local residents in Pudong and Puxi to make way for the urban infrastructures and the high-rises for accumulating capital. In other words, in the conceptual plans of making a global city, the lived space of everyday life is either subsumed under or subordinated to the conceived space. In spite of the initiative to build Shanghai as a global city, the result shows that the development plans submitted by the "global intelligence corps" call for projects of building it like other global cities, without much attention to the lived space. Likewise, municipal officials, in reviewing the layout of Pudong, specify such "'modern' areas to be orientated around the needs of the automobile" (Olds 1995: 1733). The question of whether most local residents can afford a car with their limited wages that do not necessarily catch up with the speed of the urban development does not seem to be taken into consideration. When one man's lived space happens to be another's global space, the former is left with little room to negotiate.

To make Pudong a mesmerizing Cinderella, 52,000 households (169,000 people) living in the 4-km^2 Lujiazui area are "moved forcibly to (predominantly) outlying suburban areas of the city" (Olds 1995: 1737).[2] An interview with the general manager of E. I. du Pont de Nemours, whose company invested $25 million in a Pudong project as early as 1990, brings to light the violence of rezoning in the name of development from the side of the service class. According to this du Pont manager, one drawback that affected their joint venture was that they "had to buy the houses of the farmers who originally lived on the land . . . . This money was used by local authorities to resettle the farmers elsewhere" (Gold 28). Reading between the lines, we can easily see that this pioneer investor in fact means to dismiss farmers' rights. It is assumed by du Pont that the farmers should have been relocated before their joint venture started and the payment made to resettle the farmers should not have been out of their pocket. In the style of "the real story of Pudong," the manager's account of how a multinational corporation like du Pont built their plant in Pudong from scratch is supposed to work as a reference or a model for potential investors. On the other hand, the farmers' story of what they thought of the relocation or the compensation for being uprooted received much less attention.

Pudong's development triggers a high demand for prime-site space on both sides of the Huangpu River; therefore, the lived space of Puxi people inevitably surrenders to accommodate the expected influx of foreign investment. A massive-scale conversion of industrial or residential areas into profitable commercial uses and the resulting construction boom mean the relocation of millions of inhabitants to the outskirts of the city. When the urban fabric has to be remodeled for the new user of the city and the capital flows, the original city-users often find themselves forced to give up their living space. Development might be the golden rule to follow, but relocation, for many residents, is not as simple as renting a moving truck and getting on the road. For one thing, being uprooted from the community one has been familiar with cannot be easily compensated for: what jackhammers and bulldozers demolish within minutes often takes generations to build (Chan 315). Sometimes there was only a short notice before the time for their alley houses to be demolished for new construction. On some other occasions, residents have to evacuate before the infrastructures of the new settlements are ready for them to move in.[3] To worsen the sting, long commutes become a daily ordeal for those who are relocated at the fringes of the city.

In fact, local people have lost their lived space to the global space: they not only find themselves resettled to the periphery of Shanghai but also entitled to a smaller place than before. The supposedly compensatory replacement for demolished housing sometimes could be both smaller and more jam-packed than the original one. As Roger Chan points out, instead of achieving the goal of renewal by thinning out the overcrowded housing, such relocation policy actually entailed high-density redevelopment and concentration of population (313). For example, the occupant of a 25–30-square-meter/person unit will be given an 11–12-square-meter/person unit in a nearby site, and a 12-square-meter/person unit if willing to be allocated to a fringe area (314). It was reported that the speedy pace of demolition and the problems of relocation gave rise to scattered protests."The authorities, however, were quick to deny such incident" (qtd. in Chan 320).

Such feeble resistance reveals that the implementation of the conceived space registers a top-to-down power intervention. One example that brings to light the powerful mobilization of state power to transform the lived space into profitable global space is the Chengdu Road Elevation Project. To link Chengdu Road to the inner-ring road system in the city so as to ease the traffic congestion, the 8.45-km-long project goes through four major districts of Shanghai. The construction requires about 180,000 households and thousands of work-units to relocate elsewhere (Wu 1369). Under the supervision of the development office and its branches in the four district offices, "site clearance was promptly achieved and the project was successfully completed within only two years" (Wu 1369–70). The redevelopment of the city that has been tearing down many of the *lilong* houses also destroys the cultural heritage that the traditional housing represents. Under the banner of development, modernization and globalization, the authorities tell those who express dissatisfaction with relocation for urban construction that they should prioritize the common good, assuring the inhabitants that "sacrifice is inevitable for the city as a whole to benefit in the long run" (Chan 315). After all, the sprawl of the glossy global space seems to be a one-way street. Seeing such immense demolition and relocation enforced by the collaboration of the state and the transnational capital, one can easily understand the nostalgia for the disappearing traditional alley houses, the predominant living space of Shanghainese till recently.[4]

Like alley houses, work-units define community for local inhabitants. The significance of work-units lies in the fact that they are not merely workplace organizations but the institutions responsible for the workers' benefits such as social welfare, housing and mortgages. Work-units used to be one with residential arrangements: workers' residences are likely to cluster around their workplace. Simultaneous with the resettlement of more and more *lilong* residents to high-rise projects is the drastically declining social function of work-units in the residents' daily life. The urban redevelopment that requires relocation of both residency and work-units results in the dissociation between inhabitants and their work-units. As seen in the Chengdu Road Project, thousands of work-units had to be resettled elsewhere for the construction. Such large-scale resettlement of work-units directly undermines the social functions of the work-units, which used to represent those affiliated local residents (Wu 1368). Furthermore, the economic open door policy that changes the socialist practices also accounts for the diminished role of the work-units for Shanghainese. As Wu argues, "[w]ith the retreat of state work-units in urban construction, the comprehensive management of local government and the new land-leasing system, *the right of controlling urban space has been transferred from work-units to local governments and then to external developers*" (1368; emphasis mine). Ironically, when Shanghai is reconnected with the world as planned, its inhabitants become alienated in one way or another from their familiar urban space.

For many workers in Shanghai, what urban redevelopment involves is not just the changing relationship with the work-units but, more devastatingly, the loss of their jobs. More often than not, for the city planners and developers to build the new Shanghai as a global financial hub, traditional, uncompetitive industries have to be "updated" by being shut down. In other words, for unskilled workers, the relocation of the work-units is often a euphemism for lay-offs. Prioritizing technology, information, telecommunications, and transportation, a global city would consider industries that facilitate capital mobilization as indispensable.[5] Meanwhile, labor-intensive or polluting factories, contradicting the new image of the city, become liquidated in no time as a consequence of economic Darwinism. No longer supported by the state, for example, about 400,000 workers (half of Shanghai's workers from the all-time prime industry, the textile factories) are said to have lost their job from 1993 onward ("Shanghai Takes Shape" 27). Specifically, "the government plans to relocate or shut down by 2010 two-thirds of the factories located within the 106 square kilometres enclosed by the city's inner ring road" (Yatsko 1996b: 59). Shanghai officials and urban planners try to convince us that the city's infrastructures can be effortlessly updated, worn-out architectures easily rebuilt; yet, how about laid-off unskilled workers? What is their chance of catching up with the global city formation? The transition from an industrial city to a global metropolis might create a high demand for the service class, but it cannot be overlooked that such urban redevelopment at the same time makes a large number of unskilled workers dispensable. When the developers are obsessed with promoting the old glories of the 1930s when Shanghai was a world-city of a kind, laid-off laborers might define "old glories" otherwise.[6]

Mirror and Mirage: Whose Global City Is It?

To attract foreign investment and further become a hub of capital flows, Shanghai is made in the image of a generic global city. Such a significant change is predictable: with the development of late capitalism, command-post cities turn out to be the strategic sites for state and multinational consortia to facilitate the mobilization of global capital. A Japanese urban geographer, Takashi Machimura, in presenting the problems of Tokyo's global city formation, quotes the urban plan of Frankfurt to show how the rhetoric of the German government strikingly echoes that of the Tokyo Metropolitan Government, which was taking pains to restructure Tokyo into a global city in the 1980s. I would like to use the same quote here to elucidate what I mean by the image of a generic global city and where Shanghai stands in the picture:

Frankfurt's significance in the network of international metropolises is growing. Global economic growth has not stopped. The upcurrent in the Asian-Pacific area can be felt in Frankfurt through growing economic contacts and establishments. And this is only part of the world that currently is in development. Financial trade has taken over the formerly leading role of commerce and drives forward the interweaving of the world economy. One of the nodes of this fabric is Frankfurt, which is on its way from a continental to an international financial center. (qtd. in Machimura 1998: 183)[7]

Interestingly, if we take out Frankfurt from the quote and ask people what they think the city in the quote refers to, the answers are likely to vary: it can be any global city in the making. In fact, the conceived urban space of Frankfurt and Tokyo also uncannily fits the profile of Shanghai's urban redevelopment in the 1990s. These cities are mirror images of one another since the capitalist space of globalization upholds the command-and-control cities as the ideal model for the production of urban space. A global city, a product of the operation of capitalism, thus changes into a projection and a prerequisite for any city that intends to ride the tides of global capital flow. At the same time,

A juxtaposition of different life styles: low-rises and high-rises in Zhabei, Shanghai.
(Picture taken by the author in January 2001)

repeating, replicating the mirror image of existing global cities as the irrefutable truth, the new urban space of Shanghai also functions as a mirror to local inhabitants. The shining global space convinces everyone that the reflection of a new life in the city is a political statement, a promise which is supposed to make the demolition, relocations and lay-offs necessary adjustments during a transitional period to a better future for whoever sees Shanghai as "my city."

In the master plan of the global city, it is assumed that there is no gap between the immediately experienced space and the conceived space. In other words, the image the inhabitant sees in the mirror of a global city for all is taken to be here-and-now reality instead of a mirage mediated through the looking glass of the conceived space. The dual nature of space to be both imaginary and real is concealed so that the conceived space can be camouflaged as the lived space. As Lefebvre reminds us,

> Under the conditions of modernity, as absolute political space extends its sway, the impression of transparency becomes stronger and stronger, and the illusion of a new life is everywhere reinforced. Real life indeed appears quite close to us. We feel able, from within everyday life, to reach out and grasp it, as though nothing lay between us and the marvellous reality on the other side of the mirror. (189)

The seemingly transparent space that reflects an image of a city of the future for all of its users is the same one that hides from sight the allocation of social resources, the one that accommodates the service class's claims to the global city at the expense of others. As the other face of "successful people" is always blurred, so the power interventions of the global city production remain elusive.[8] Maybe there is a reason for so many skyscrapers to be made of glass: one thinks one can see through the transparent glass of the buildings, but what one sees is only mesmerizing reflection and mirage. What appears to be crystal clear is paradoxically the most opaque, the operation of capital mobilization.

8
Sleeping Beauty Waking Up to a New World of Capital:
Wang Anyi's Shanghai Stories

Reminding everyone of its time as the Paris of the Orient in the 1930s, Shanghai's global-city formation turns the city once again into a shining star on the international stage. Parallel to the large-scale construction of the city of tomorrow, in the political and urban discourse there is an appeal to pick up the threads and regain the splendor of Old Shanghai. Such rhetoric is by no means coincidental: I would like to argue that the glory of Old Shanghai, a leitmotif in the urban discourse of Shanghai's global spatialization, is a powerful and convenient mirage produced by the new global space of the city. The mirror image, presented by the global-city campaign for its onlookers to identify with, is Janus-faced, one side advertising the ultramodern skyline in Pudong, and the other the historical Shanghai as a big city with bright lights and urban legends of all kinds.[1]

Incorporated in the place-making narrative, the city's history and traditions are reflected as a coded image for its inhabitants to relate to the present redevelopment and, by extension, to the global future. Shanghai's past is re-evoked as a collective dream to make the present fantasy land of global sublime a credible story and tangible reality for everyone. The reconstruction of Shanghai in the 1990s is often spuriously celebrated as a Sleeping Beauty story.[2] Notably, what is often evoked as unforgettable is Shanghai during the 1920s and 1930s, the time when the city was a cosmopolitan metropolis, rather than the years between 1949 and the end of the Cultural Revolution in 1976. Such nostalgia, "Forward to the Past" in Ackbar Abbas's words, functions to expedite global capital accumulation (2000: 780). It seems that as long as one can find traces of the past in what points to the future, like the new Lujiazui financial center as an extension of the Bund, the here-and-now construction everywhere in the city will appear fine. The glamour of the global city is in fact both seductive and illusory. The image of a phantasmagoric Old Shanghai, in the manner of a Hollywood diva like Greta Garbo, re-enchants the foreign investors and the local residents with a cosmopolitan past as not only a cultural heritage but also the foundation for the global city.

In the following discussion, I intend to explore the ideological complexity implied in the discourse of remembering the Old Shanghai by examining novelist Wang Anyi's works. For Wang, the essence of the glory lies in the seemingly insignificant details of life, which are the most solid foundation of the global sublime, indispensable and indestructible, however overshadowed by the facile splendor of the new urban space. In this sense, her works, fictional or not, typify the urban discourse of rebuilding the glory of the Old Shanghai in modern times. Yet, while Wang on the one hand foregrounds the unassailable banality of Shanghai's glory, she also narrates the anxiety over the disappearing alley houses and the details of Shanghai life as she remembers them. I argue that such ambivalence toward the contemporary Shanghai cityscape as seen in Wang's writings becomes a strategic site for examining the contradictions engendered by the formation of the global city. Even as she cogently grasps the changes that have turned Shanghai into a global city, Wang unwittingly reinforces the image-making mechanism, the precondition for producing a capitalist space.

Mirage of Old Shanghai: "Meitou" and *The Song of Unending Sorrow*[3]

The novella "Meitou" demonstrates a pattern of reconnecting Shanghai with its present development as a global city. Wang Anyi supplements the abstract global space by summoning up the details of old *lilong* life as the matrix of a new Shanghai and envisioning pedestrians' faces as the landmarks of the city. Centering on a couple named Meitou and Xiaobai, the story tells of urban life in *lilong* housing on Huai Hai Road from the time of the Cultural Revolution to the era of globalization. The daily updated urban landscape mirrors the characters' new life away from their roots, the *lilong* community. Notably, when the characters' encounters over the years are rendered as success stories composed of chance and hard work, the urban transformation becomes naturalized as a sensible course to take as well.

By characterizing how the female protagonist Meitou dexterously deals with details of everyday life, Wang dramatizes Shanghai's development into a global city. As the story unfolds, we see Meitou walking through the turbulent years of the Cultural Revolution, growing up from a next-door girl in the *lilong* neighborhood to a housewife and mother. By chance, she partners with her childhood neighbor in the fashion industry in Guangdong, having an affair during a business trip and emigrating to Buenos Aires after the divorce. Xiaobai's life also reveals the urban change of the city: leaving their *lilong* house, he moves to one high-rise after another in the new areas of the city. The present urban image is rendered comprehensible because of the reader's identification with the characters and the linearity of the narrative. At the end of the story, through Xiaobai's walking on Huai Hai road and his sense of loss upon seeing the homogeneous faces of the crowd, Wang repeatedly invokes the phantom of the past to complete the image of the globalized Shanghai:

> Now, walking on the bustling street, what strikes him [Xiaobai] as most impressive is the pretty women, who unanimously model the latest fashion. Fashion makes these women resemble one another. It is not like before when girls on every street all look different. Each street has its specific pretty faces. (2001: 166)

Superimposing the global image of Shanghai onto the characters rooted in Old Shanghai, Wang vicariously gives the alien forces of globalization a familiar and vernacular look. The homogeneous crowd once again suddenly changes to those familiar faces that Xiaobai remembers, and among them, he sees the face of his ex-wife Meitou, who walks in the crowd and then flies away, leaving all the faces behind her all the way to Buenos Aires (2001: 168). As suggested in Xiaobai's vision of her flying, Meitou transforms herself from a *longtang* girl into a successful transnational business woman. Her change not only allegorizes Shanghai's transformation but also hints at the link between the disappeared Shanghai and the global city in the making. I argue that the plot of Meitou in a sense endorses the urban history of global-city formation. When Meitou no longer walks on Huai Hai road but flies away to the most foreign city imaginable, the story implicitly suggests the success of Shanghai as a symbol of global financial take-off, embodied by the most concrete and realistic lived space of alley houses. "Meitou" thus speaks for an endeavor to displace the anxiety over the disappearing lived space of Shanghai resulted from the accelerating pace of globalization onto a detailed representation of *lilong* life at the time around the Cultural Revolution.

In *The Song of Unending Sorrow*, generally considered one of Wang's best works, one sees a similar, but much more ambitious, attempt to rescue the remains of Old Shanghai and compose with fragmentary images a representation of how Shanghai and Shanghai life should be perceived today despite the demolition frenzy and construction boom.[4] It seems that as long as the novelist can tell a story of where Shanghai comes from and what the city goes through, the riddle of where Shanghai is going to after a decade of massive urban redevelopment can be solved.

For Wang Anyi, "the legend of Wang Qiyao [the female protagonist] is Shanghai's dream of glory. The glory and the dream might be old, but the luster will shine through for another half century" (2000: 151). Shanghai's glamour finds its foundation in the alley houses and thus has everything to do with daily life. The reason why the space of *lilongs* pulls the heartstrings is because of its tangibility: "*Longtangs* in Shanghai are sexy: one feels as intimate to the space as to one's own body, as if *longtang*'s warmth and coldness are tangible." "The back lanes of *lilongs* are winding into people's hearts." In short,

> the emotional power of alley houses lies in the sights and sounds of everyday life... It is not the power of the heroic epic, but that of the accumulation of details of the most ordinary life. Flowing among those lines of houses is nothing grand, but as minute as grains of sand, which can build a tower when brought together. That has nothing to do with such things as history, not even unofficial history, maybe the best name for such narrative is gossip (流言) ... But such gossip also bears the imprints of time — as intimate as our skin even if it is idle. (2000: 20)

Gossip turns the urban legend of Shanghai into the "Paris of the East" (2000: 23). The above quote on details and gossip demonstrates clearly the author's emphasis on the importance of "little narratives," stories of ordinary people's everyday lives. Wang believes that such diminutive details are the most solid ground of urban life.

In the novel, Wang Qiyao signifies the bridge of Shanghai's past and present precisely because she embodies the sensuous details of Shanghai life in alley houses, the spectacular-in-banality, which for the author is everything particular about Shanghai's charms. Wang Qiyao's story dramatizes the changes of Shanghai over decades through the ups and downs in this fictional character's lifetime. It is no accident that the novel narrates the story of a girl from *longtang* turning into a gorgeous Miss Shanghai, a kept-woman in the mistress apartment, and then a single mother back in *longtang*. The female protagonist is introduced to the reader as a type rather than an individual, that of "the daughter of alley houses," the personification of "little narratives," in this case, details of life and widespread gossip. Throughout the novel, Miss Shanghai, Wang Qiyao, undoubtedly functions as the alternative but authentic image of Shanghai that Wang Anyi is eager to present. I would like to explore how Wang Qiyao is not only a synecdoche for Shanghai glamour rooted in *longtangs* (protagonist as a mirror image created by the author), but also a medium through which the images of Old Shanghai are reflected (protagonist as a looking glass). The characterization of Wang Qiyao is, in short, a site of contradiction. Wang Anyi on the one hand employs her as the center of nostalgia in the novel, but the author at the same time criticizes the other characters' emotional investment in Wang Qiyao as an object of the memorabilia of the past.

By coincidence, the school-girl Wang Qiyao first becomes a poster girl for a magazine called *Shanghai Life*, shot by an amateur photographer, Mr. Cheng, and then becomes Miss Shanghai in the beauty pageant. The outcome of the spectacular Miss Shanghai campaign, the turning-point in Wang Qiyao's life, is that she ranks as the third, nicknamed as "Miss Number Three." Again, Wang Qiyao is no queen who will be the protagonist of a heroic epic, but the much downplayed allure nurtured by the routine life in *lilongs*:

> Wang Qiyao ranked third in the campaign. . . . Miss Number Three is indispensable. . . . We might as well say that she represents the majority, the quiet crowds that set the key tone of the sensual city. Those walkers on the street are Miss Number Threes. Misses Number One and Two are social butterflies that one rarely sees other than in some major events. *Yet Miss Number Three is the familiar scenery of everyday life that warms our hearts. Miss Number Three in fact represents the populist will. While Misses Number One and Two are idols, our ideals and convictions, Miss Number Three is tied up with our ordinary days.* (2000: 80; emphasis mine)

This quote specifically reveals the symbolic relationships between Wang Qiyao and the daily life of Shanghai.[5] While the lingering image of Shanghai invites us to see the city as a seductive diva like Miss Number One or Miss Number Two, Wang Anyi endeavors to show us what she calls the "core" or "essence" of the apparent charms of Wang Qiyao/Shanghai. Without the root or source of mundane *lilong* life, the enchantment of the beauty/city is at best an inaccessible mirage, a sheer Vanity Fair that satisfies the eyes but not the heart. Miss Number Three later becomes the mistress of Mr. Li, a high-power politician, and moves to the fancy Alice Apartment. Her days as a kept woman end with the Communist take-over in 1949 after Mr. Li died in a plane crash. Wang Qiyao from then on lives at Ping An Li, a not-so-glamorous *longtang*, where she makes a living as a door-to-door nurse and later becomes a single mother. It is noteworthy that the name of this *lilong* is not randomly chosen. For one thing, Ping An means safe and secure, thus giving an ironic twist for the mishap at the end of the story. Moreover, the fact that there are many *longtangs* named Ping An Li in Shanghai suggests that like Wang Qiyao, Ping An Li is an archetypal residential complex and Wang Anyi is telling a story of "everyman" at every *lilong* of Shanghai.

In narrating the ups and downs in the life of Miss Number Three, Wang Anyi repeatedly shows her protagonist's reflection in a mirror or in the water to suggest that Miss Number Three *is* Shanghai and vice versa. The identification of the protagonist and the image of Shanghai is made through the mirror effects of both the looking glass and the surface of the river. Significantly, the absent Shanghai becomes the double of Wang Qiyao: where she is supposed to see her own reflection, she sees the city as remembered instead. Several examples of Wang Qiyao looking into the mirror help us see the identification of the protagonist and the image of Shanghai. At Wuqiao, a small water town where her grandmother lives, Wang Qiyao sees the Shanghai that she has left physically after her lover's untimely death but can never leave behind emotionally. Wherever she goes, the image of Shanghai haunts her:

> In the morning she sees Shanghai in the mirror while combing her hair. But that Shanghai is somewhat weary, some fine lines can be found under the eyes. Walking along the river, she sees the reflection of Shanghai in the water. That Shanghai's bright colors have faded. . . . She cannot bear to think about the city. Every thought would trigger acute pains. . . . Shanghai is incredible — how can one forget its splendor, which shines through even after everything is gone. The luster can still pierce all. (2000: 158)

Unable to live apart from her reflection, Miss Shanghai has to return to the city even though her wound is not healed. Back in the alley houses, persuaded by her new friend, Mrs. Yan, Wang Qiyao walks into the beauty parlor to have a perm. In the shop, where everything feels so familiar to her, once again Wang looks into the mirror and sees an image of herself, a self not as she is now but the way she was in the past (2000: 168). At another time, Mrs.

Yan takes Wang to her house and shows her in front of the mirror in her bedroom a piece of red textile for making a coat. Wang Qiyao sees in the looking glass the reflection of her past, this time a pipe on the headboard of the bed, which reminds her of the Alice Apartment and her old days as a mistress (2000: 172). Wang Qiyao, as these examples suggest, is inseparable from the mirror image, an image fossilized in time.

Wang Anyi also fossilizes the city by monumentalizing details of everyday life in Old Shanghai, which remain intact regardless of the political agitation. An example can be seen in the regular gatherings of Wang Qiyao, Mrs. Yan, her cousin Kang Mingxun and his Russian-Chinese friend Sasha during the time of the Anti-Rightists Campaign. These four gather on a daily basis in Wang Qiyao's living room, either for afternoon tea or a meal. Over delicious dishes and various desserts prepared by Wang Qiyao, they play cards or mahjong, chat or tell jokes with the blue flames of Wang's oil lamp dancing on the table and the heater warming everyone in the room. Cataloguing what the men and women eat and drink, how they entertain one another with games and conversations, Wang Anyi elaborates the details of their routine party against the downplayed background of political turbulence. Who would think people can lead such a charmed life at the time of the Anti-Rightists Movement? The narrator describes the discrepancy between the undisturbed space of Wang Qiyao's living room and the city:

> It is the winter of 1957. A lot of commotion took place in the outside world but that has nothing to do with the small world next to the furnace. This small world sits at the edge of the universe or in a tiny crevice. They [the small world and the universe] forget each other and that makes the small world safe. Outside it is snowing, but there is a hot stove in the house. What a beautiful time! They cook so many different things over the stove. They come in the morning, eating and chatting all day till dawn. The sun is invisible on snowy days and even the flow of time becomes indiscernible. Upon leaving at night, they seem to be half-dreaming. (2000: 192)

Again, foregrounding Wang Qiyao, the author presents the *carpe diem* aura of an alternative world, a secret Shanghai composed of seemingly insignificant trivia of ordinary people's concrete space of everyday life that somehow magically remains in one piece. For Wang Anyi the power of such fragments or trivia lies in the fact that they are the foundation of things: "The food over the stove gives out little noises and indistinguishable scents, filling out the gaps in the world. The whole brick or whole rock of the world is made sturdy because of these little nothings" (2000: 198–9). These dust-like little nothings are atoms, extremely small but irreducible and indestructible material units. The totality of these atoms of everyday life is Wang Anyi's eternal Shanghai.

Wang Qiyao, the synonym for everyday life in *longtangs*, the authentic Shanghai, functions as the author's medium to the disappearing Shanghai, as the mirror through which the images of the enchanting city become accessible and concrete both for the characters and the reader. The magic wand of daily life transforms Shanghai from a legend in the other life or life of the others into a personal diary of everyone who is ready to call Shanghai "my city." For the characters in the novel, Wang Qiyao is the looking glass that turns everything into a scrap of memorabilia that seemingly allows one to be reconnected with the past.[6]

Wang Qiyao as a Shanghai double allures her male companions to project her as a mirror of the city's old glory. To be with Wang Qiyao often means returning to the bygone Shanghai, a time travel that they come to recognize in the end as illusory and ephemeral. The case in point is the character Old Color, Wang Qiyao's last prince charming, whose nickname signifies his predilection for the memorabilia related to Old Shanghai.[7] Wang Anyi suggests the pitfall of falling for the obvious magnificence of Shanghai but not the timeless everyday life in *lilongs* by detailing the relationship between Wang Qiyao and this nostalgic 26-year-old school teacher, who adores nothing more than his own city in the 1940s.

Old Color is one significant type in Wang Anyi's portrait gallery, a "face" (臉相) that one bumps into on the street in contemporary Shanghai. As a *flâneur*, he walks in the city to indulge in nostalgia:

> The streets in the West side of the city know Old Color best. He frequents there from time to time. . . . Mao Ming Road changes from a busy street to a quiet area, both the noise and the tranquility have histories of themselves. Old Color loves walking there, travelling back in time. . . . The East side streets also know him very well. . . . Every street leads to the bank of the Huangpu River. . . . The flying seagulls are timeless, just like the pigeons — timeless, exactly what he wants. (2000: 343)

Walking enables Old Color to imagine that he can be reconnected with Old Shanghai, the city that he perceives as eternal regardless of the urban redevelopment of his time.

The urban reconstruction that accelerated in Shanghai in the 1980s becomes a seedbed for the rise of a new-generation of nostalgic urbanites, who share the desperate attempt to grasp every residue of the Old Shanghai ambience. They are the loyal proponents for the "old fashion." It seems only natural for such types of characters to be drawn to Wang Qiyao, the epitome of what the nostalgic mind is pining for: aging but luminous, irreplaceable by any modern simulation. At first, Old Color is charmed by Wang Qiyao, identifying her as the symbol of the timeless Old Shanghai splendor. The moment he sees Wang Qiyao at a party, Old Color imagines that for the first time in his life he has come face to face with "the essence of the old time," in sharp contrast with his previous experiences of being lost "among its shallow imitations" (2000: 347). The appearance of Wang Qiyao in his life seems to empower Old Color to complete a personal vision of 1940s' Shanghai: "he suspected he is in fact a reincarnation of a person who died in an accident 40 years ago. Unable to leave behind what he has been attached to in the previous life, he comes back to pick up the loose threads." He fantasizes himself to have been a typical clerk, working in a trading firm (洋行), killed in an accident in the cable car on his way to work (2000: 348). Upon listening to her life story in the once-upon-a-time Shanghai, Old Color sees Wang's face as "unreal as the reflection in the water," weeping and lamenting "where is the beginning of the story? Even if she is telling a sad story, it is a grandiose tragedy. How would the story end?" (2000: 373–4)

For Old Color, Wang Qiyao might concretize the good old days that no old jazz can ever do for him, but what he wants from the aged Miss Shanghai is a reenactment of the drama with Wang Qiyao as the diva and himself as a loyal fan. Their relationship reveals Wang Qiyao and the Old Shanghai she represents as abstract and frozen in time:

> It [Wang's old wooden box] is a good prop for him to immerse himself in that 40s show. More or less, he sees Wang Qiyao as the Hollywood diva. . . . But he plays the role of her number-one fan... He can never be tired of watching . . . Sometimes he is too engrossed in the show to remember where he is. (2000: 353)

One moment at Wang's place, upon seeing the flickering light of the coal fire dance over her face, Old Color realized that "[s]he is an old lady." (2000: 371) Even at the moment of making love to her, Wang Qiyao, "a silhouette of another world," seems to be neither concrete nor real, the extreme opposite of the lived space of everyday life that Wang Qiyao signifies (2000: 377). When Wang Qiyao can only serve as the eternal drama for Old Color, she inevitably becomes the force that dissociates him from his routine life. Walking on the street after leaving Wang's Ping An Li the night after having sex with her, Old Color ponders if he is sleepwalking. His moment of ecstasy is mingled with incubus. The narrator describes Old Color as being haunted by nightmares:

> Every evening he cannot help but head for Wang's as if invited by those nightmares. He cannot remember the last time he went to a record store or how long he has been away from his music. The records he collected are now all dusty... He has no choice but to go to Wang Qiyao's place, where new nightmares are born. (2000: 378)

It is at the swimming pool of a hotel which Old Color used to frequent that he finally comes to understand that Wang, the fascinating living Old Shanghai, for him means not only an impossible future but a present uprooted from the earth of his own ordinary life. The awareness comes from the immediacy experienced through the body in motion: "He swims back and forth in the pool. . . . It feels good to have the water running over the body, telling you the power and elasticity of the body. . . . Some confusion inside becomes clarified through exercise. *Now he can think*" (2000: 387; emphasis mine). Old Color leaves the pool, taking the elevator in the hotel down to the street-level. Seeing the city shining with lights from inside the elevator, Old Color remembers Wang Qiyao sitting quietly at the corner of a party. The narrator reveals the unsaid awakening: "Old Color is probably more obsessed with the good old days of 40 years ago than anyone else, but the heart pounding in his body is a heart of here-and-now" (2000: 387). The novel seems to suggest that the problem with the nostalgia as illustrated by Old Color is that his fetish for the luminous mirage of Old Shanghai drives him to identify Wang Qiyao with the drama and thus reduces her to a flat character rather than a real person in his daily life. Wang Qiyao once tells Old Color what the essence of Old Shanghai should be like — the art of leading everyday life whole-heartedly: "40 years ago Shanghai was a cosmopolitan world where you found kaleidoscopic scenery. Yet, it is important to draw the line between scenes outside the window and what lies inside it: the base of and key to everyday life" (2000: 349). Ironically, it is when Old Color starts to draw the line between drama and real life that he drifts away.

In fact, Old Color's refusal of Wang Qiyao can also be seen in a different light. Old Color's romance with Wang Qiyao hinges on his falling for the mirror image of Old Shanghai drama, while his farewell to Miss Shanghai is an indication of seeing the medium of the image. In other words, if Wang Qiyao is "the flower in the mirror and the moon on the water" (鏡花水月), Old Color tends to see "flower and moon" at the beginning of their relationship, which ends at the moment when he sees only the mirror and the water. When Old Color's attention is brought to the medium of the fantastic reflection of Wang Qiyao/Old Shanghai, he refuses to walk through the looking glass and become a lived abstraction as Alice does (Lefebvre 314). Saying no to Wang Qiyao in this sense is a rejection of the fossilized history of Old Shanghai.

The unhappy ending between Wang Qiyao and Old Color imparts a problematics of history and everyday life. After all, what can one do to continue the details of everyday life, for life in Old Shanghai to become one with that of the current global city? Wang Anyi raises this important question by insisting on the necessity of laying the foundation of the future Shanghai with details of everyday life handed down from the Shanghai of yesterday. Nevertheless, as shown in the story of Wang Qiyao and Old Color, the novel does not address this problematics adequately but rather leaves it dangling in the air.

What is absent from Wang Qiyao's frustrated relationship with Old Color is the crisis of what she represents in the contemporary era, specifically, the *lilong* life in today's Shanghai. Not only is the true value of the details of daily life overshadowed by the apparent splendor but also the space that nurtures such a careful and elaborate life style is threatened by extinction. With the large-scale urban redevelopment, the alley housing like Wang Qiyao's Ping An Li is disappearing at a speedy pace. More than once in the last part of the novel *lilongs* are compared to a sunken ship: "Oh, this city is like a sunken ship. The utility poles are the masts of the ship. The cloud above the ship is what sustains the illusion, a mirage. The noises of stomping stakes echo each other as if to stomp the whole city to the underground" (2000: 353). Toward the end of the novel, the narrator says, "The pigeons are singing an elegy for the old city. Among the new buildings these old alley houses are like buried shipwrecks. When the tides ebb, the skeletons are exposed" (2000: 397–8). If we read Wang's description against Roger Chan's article on the problems brought about by the urban renewal in Shanghai mentioned earlier, we see that the new threat to Ping An Li acquires a very specific form: the demolition of the alley houses. Thus, we have to interpret Old Color's refusal of Wang Qiyao as an articulation of the political unconscious, a half-revealed awareness of the historical crisis in the development of Shanghai as a global city. The disappearance of solid, sensuous and intimate community life is analogous to Old Color's individual rejection of the details of everyday life that Wang Qiyao is supposed to represent. Toward the end of the story, we catch a glimpse of the fearful destruction of everyday life as an undesirable consequence of globalizing Shanghai. In the penultimate chapter, the narrator describes a lurking danger that cannot be put into words: "all the lights behind the windows are frightened peoples' alert eyes looking for the sources of danger. But when true danger comes close, none of them hear its footsteps. . . . They are not prepared for any kind of danger outside of what they have learned from life experiences" (2000: 368).

The massive destruction of Old Shanghai parallels the protagonist's impending doom, brought about by the character Long Leg. While Long Leg is fascinated with the new look of the global city, by the end of the novel he turns out to be the murderer of Miss Shanghai. This foil character of Old Color illustrates Wang Anyi's political unconscious of Shanghai as a global city in two senses. For one thing, the impulsive murder allegorizes the confrontation between the everyday life in *lontangs* (embodied by Wang Qiyao) and the global dream, positing it as the most rootless and thus dangerous glory (embodied by Long Leg).

At the same time, the unflattering representation of Long Leg can be seen as the author's repression of the image of the global city as a dual city. Introduced to the reader as one of the boyfriends of Zhang Yonghong, a girlfriend of Wang Qiyao's daughter, Long Leg is later presented as a migrant, a small-timer-passed-as-successful-man. Notably, unlike Old Color, a native of *lilong*, Long Leg is blind to the splendor of Old Shanghai perhaps because he is a migrant to the city, who does everything to assimilate himself to the urban landscape, only to become a pseudo success.[8] The author suggests through Long Leg's example that what appears to be the *most* global is ironically the most provincial.

The detailed account of Long Leg's global dream serves to expose the fallacy of endorsing the glittering façade of Shanghai. Falling for the image of the global city, Long Leg sees himself as part of the dazzling global city and re-inscribes the lingering myth of Old Shanghai as the hometown of the self-made millionaire on his vitae. In fact, his family history is the Arabian Nights enabled by the new Shanghai ready for the global era. Trying to convince everyone around him that the whole globe is his backyard, Long Leg tells

Zhang Yonghong that he is the only grandson, the legal heir to a famous soy sauce entrepreneur in Old Shanghai. According to him, "grandpa's soy sauce factories are all over Southeast Asia and some in Europe and America. Besides the soy sauce industry, he had rubber tree farm, plantations and even forests. Their family had a private harbor dock on the Mekong River in Vietnam and Wall Street sells his stocks" (2000: 356). Whenever Long Leg is short of money and has to hide, he tells everyone that he has to go out of town to see relatives coming back to visit from abroad. For example, it is rumored that Long Leg goes to Hong Kong when people don't see him for a few days after the Chinese New Year. They say that he is not going to come back to Shanghai since his cousin has managed to help him emigrate to Hong Kong. Some other people say that the purpose of his trip is to take care of his inheritance (2000: 386). When Long Leg shows up again after his alleged Hong Kong trip, he meets with Zhang Yonghong at a café and tells her everything about Hong Kong. The narrator portrays Long Leg's global dream as such: "How clearly can he see the city! Then here comes the bright future for both of them — they will have a big wedding in Bangkok or San Francisco" (2000: 390). For Wang Anyi, Long Leg's global myth, a hybrid of the long-standing urban legend of Old Shanghai and the highly promoted small-world-global-village image, is the most glaring contrast to the sensible, down-to-earth life style of *lilongs*.

It would be instructive to read the characterization of Long Leg against the narrative intention. According to René Girard, scapegoating is a very important act in mimesis. If this is true, we might say without a doubt that Long Leg is a scapegoat that makes Wang Anyi's representation of Shanghai possible. Making a living by playing tennis with foreigners, teaching them how to ride a motorcycle, showing visitors around in the city, and exchanging foreign currency, people like Long Leg might look "international." Long Leg's story shows us what lurks beneath the glittering surface. When people are gossiping about his trip to Hong Kong, Long Leg is in fact riding in a make-shift truck in bitter winter days to Hong Ze Lake in the neighboring province to sell seafood. Hanging out at the space of the city's fashionable restaurants or hotel lobbies, Long Leg still has to go back at night to his shabby home in a slum-like area of the city, where he finds leftovers to eat if he is lucky. The "successful man" walking on the Huai Hai Road is in fact less than nobody. Desperate to be seen as a real Shanghainese of his time, by Long Leg's definition, a man empowered by money, mobilization, and global connections, he has no life other than the social life, identical with the nightlife of the "successful man" in the metropolis.

The images of the two expanding classes in the city, the service class and the migrant laborers, are condensed into Long Leg, the arch villain in the story and the enemy of the everyday life Wang Anyi endeavors to revive. Because Long Leg is a fake thus his presence conceals the uneven development engendered by the new urban morphology of the global city. To fill out the gap of the abstract space of the global city, Wang essentializes Shanghai, ontologizing the everyday life in *lilongs* to such a point that the details of everyday life become ahistorical and self-contained. This partly accounts for why one cannot see how international business people demand that the *lilong* inhabitants relocate to more remote locations to help centralize the global capital and the infrastructure which supports it. At the same time, we cannot see how the urban migrant laborers construct the city from the ground up, constructing temples of affluence for the super-wealthy, but do not partake of their own superfluous creation, a creation whose illusion of abundance depends on their own labor. In short, neither the lived space of the service class nor that of the migrant laborers is represented. Yet, one of the keys to comprehending the source of the endless sorrows of Wang Qiyao in contemporary Shanghai is exactly the on-going negotiation among the lived space of these two absent classes and that of the inhabitants of *longtangs*. Long Leg's double life is ironically the discursive move for the author to provide an imaginary solution to the narrative of the novel. In order to assume that one can see the city in its entirety, Long Leg is posed as the blind man who cannot see the supposed "essence" of Shanghai, the details of everyday life of Shanghai, which Wang Qiyao embodies in many ways as discussed earlier. In the novel Long Leg is a "worm moving in a tomb," idling in the daytime (2000: 358), and the "murkiest point on the margin of the city's halo, that is why he cannot see himself" (2000: 389). His murder of Wang Qiyao suggests allegorically that he is not able to see the essence of the city and actually hides the blindness of those who fail to see the enemy of the daily life, the rapid demolition and reconstruction of Shanghai brought about by the concentration of global capital. Let us recall here that one fifth of the heavy-weight construction cranes are in Shanghai for the global-city campaign. Long Leg is the scapegoat that deflects one's attention from the causes of urban changes in Shanghai.

Looking for Shanghai: Meandering on Foot in a Labyrinthian City of Mirrors

Wang Anyi has been determinedly undertaking the Herculean task of bridging the gap between the lived space and the conceived space of Shanghai as a global city. Her essay "Looking for Shanghai" can be read as an expression of her longing to reclaim "her" city, a city that is on the verge of disappearing forever. It is an illustration of how the author accesses the image of Old Shanghai to complement the seemingly omnipresent monumental space as a result of globalization. Wang says,

> In a nutshell, Shanghai is not sensual any more. New buildings construct a new cover for it, which separates the city from the physical senses of its inhabitants. Such a fancy cover, however, does not fit perfectly. *There is always some empty space in between the exterior and the real thing.* Or maybe it is due to the fact that we are too close to the city and it happens to undergo drastic changes. All the visions are blurred. In the end, only some after-images can be grasped. (2001: 221; emphasis mine)

For Wang, it seems that the way to make the new cover of the city feel right is to fill out the void between the fancy exterior and its core. However, such an attempt would leave unchallenged the major cause of hollowing out the lived experiences, the already constructed high-rises that have replaced *lilong* housing on a large scale and at a rapid rate. Wang Anyi assumes that the exterior of Shanghai is already under construction and the task left is to substantiate the new Shanghai with details of everyday life. The complicated interaction between the lived space and the conceived space thus becomes unexplored.

In this essay, walking is of great importance in furnishing the details the new city lacks. Walking as a daily practice that allows Wang to explore the urban space bodily empowers her to bring herself closer to the memories of sensuous details of the city, which represent the disappeared Old Shanghai. Seeing the newly developed streets in Shanghai, Wang laments in a matter-of-fact tone that "[a]t that time, there were plenty of different faces in this street. Now everyone looks the same. In the past, every visage accompanied a particular demeanor, which made the face stand out in the crowd" (2001: 211). Walking on the street, strange to say, becomes a way of not seeing the new cityscape. On the trendy but homogeneous faces of the street crowd, Wang sees those faces she remembers. One example of such unforgettable faces is that of a typical female owner of a tobacco shop-front. The small drugstore keepers all have such a stern visage with an oval face, bulging eyes and thick lips. In a manner of physiognomy, Wang describes the woman's face and the associated profession in detail to further present the space she stands for. The singled-out face in the crowd is the medium that helps Wang envision the disappeared life style and urban space:

> Such types of small drugstores are magic spaces protruding from the walls of one's homes facing the street [Huai Hai Road]. This is the marvelous part of the street. Among the fancy stores are residential housing, and behind the stores are labyrinthian populous alley houses. (2001: 206)

The sad face of an old man is another reference point on the map of Wang's Old Shanghai. Tinged with a melancholy aura behind the neon lights and busy shops, this sad face belongs to the one that earns his living by bringing people buckets of hot water in winter (Lao Hu Zao, hot water station), a profession that also relies on the community of *lilongs*, specifically the public space at the lane corners. With *longtangs*, the urban space that such walks of life rely on, gradually fade out of the Shanghainese's vision; such faces and the slice of community life they represent vanish in real life but reappear in the mirror of nostalgia.[9] For Wang, walking is to associate once again the unfamiliar new cityscape with something old, borrowed from memories.

Wang's grand project to bridge the gap between the disappearing local and the newly built global deserves compliments and admiration, but we cannot help noticing a fundamental limitation in such a project, a pattern found prevalent in the discourse of nostalgia craze for the Old Shanghai. That is, it is the mirror image of Old Shanghai within that of Shanghai as a global city that drives Wang Anyi to present Old Shanghai from an insider's perspective. Wang's continuous efforts at anchoring Shanghai's image on the details of everyday life to make the mirage of global city seem accessible often turns out to be frustrating and melancholic experiences since the evoked phantom of the daily life cannot replace the continuously shrinking and disappearing concrete space of everyday life at the present moment. The authentic Shanghai that supposedly works as a supplement to the homogenizing space of the global city has already been reduced to nothing more than flat, stereotyped images for public consumption.

The problematics of Wang Anyi's quest for Shanghai, i.e., to complete the missing piece of her global city with nuances of urban life as she remembers, is evident in the incongruous ending of this essay, in which the narrator contemplates the future Shanghai while seeing the spectacle of Hong Kong. Sitting leisurely at the Regent Hotel in Kowloon in 1997, Wang sees the dazzling Hong Kong Island shining in the sea under the jet-black sky. This window scene of Hong Kong, narrated as a legend of "civilization born out of a barren island," reminds her of the genesis of Shanghai in a book on the city's archaeology. She exclaims, "What a spectacular scene! Shanghai rises from the ocean slowly. With the fogs disappearing, the city seems to be closer and closer. I walk into what I see, buried by detailed descriptions of the city, and finally everything becomes indiscernible" (2001: 222).

This ending of unexpectedly finding Shanghai in Hong Kong is inconsistent with her previous lament that new city layouts have eliminated old shops and heterogeneous faces. What intrigues me here is how Wang's vision of Hong Kong helps us understand the political unconscious of Shanghai's globalization in the discourse of Shanghai nostalgia. To Wang Anyi, the conceived space of Shanghai is no more than a composite of high-rises and concrete, an imaginary container to be filled up with details of everyday life. In this sense, Wang unknowingly perpetuates the fetish of space. As Lefebvre argues, the central problematics of city-building in the contemporary world is to think of the realms of everyday life as empty containers (296–7). As discussed earlier, the response to globalization from a walker's vantage point reveals the gap between local people's life in the city and the global sublime they are supposed to identify with. The sensuous details, the concrete space of everyday life or "representational space" in Lefebvre's words, serve as a counterpart to the rational representation of space. It is through walking that Wang allows us to see the divergence between these two perceptions of space. However, it is Hong Kong, another space of globalization, that enables her to see Shanghai, now a global city in the making. One should notice Wang's vision of the double images of the two global cities conveys a strong sense of admiration on her part. While she strenuously endeavors to show the world an authentic Shanghai that differs from its new fashionable look, Wang ironically endorses the stereotype of Hong Kong as a legend of capital. She sees Hong Kong from a tourist's perspective in a very tourist corner of a five-star hotel, itself one of the quintessential spaces of globalization. Abstracting Hong Kong to a flat image of "civilization born on a barren island," Wang remains uncritical of the possible tension between the local and the global in Hong Kong's urban space.

The montage of Hong Kong and Shanghai as described at the end of the author's quest is by no means an accident, but a revealing example of the far-reaching effects of global mirage. Wang subscribes to the mirror image of Hong Kong as a global city without being critically aware that there might also be divergence between Hong Kong as a global city, the Pearl of the Orient, and Hong Kong as experienced sensually by local people. When Wang stops walking and thereby detaches herself from the details of Shanghai life, the political unconscious, a latent desire to articulate the tension between the local present and the global future imparted throughout this prose, is kept at bay.

Wang's uncritical representation of Hong Kong's global space contrasts sharply with what she has been endeavoring to do in her fictional narratives: earnestly dramatize Old Shanghai, monumentalize details of everyday life and call forth phantoms of the past as a means of complementing the current urban life of global Shanghai. Her different cognitive mappings of these two global cities suggest the power of the global city mirage to seduce city-users into seeing the conceived space as the lived space as demonstrated in Wang's montage of seeing Shanghai in Hong Kong. Wang's writings also point to the double-bind of resorting to imaginary details of life in the past as a remedy to on-going urban redevelopment. Without a critical distance, the memories of Old Shanghai invoked by the author could easily turn into stock images available for capital consumption, and thus facilitate the expansion of abstract space, which has resulted in the rapid destruction of the Shanghai way of life the author hopes to preserve.

When relocation of the inhabitants as required by the re-zoning of the global city becomes a shared experience for most Shanghainese, it is understandable that the reference points for Wang to map the city, the visage of walks of life, turn out to be phantoms of the old days in a lost space. With the space that produces the most quintessential Shanghai spirit, *lilong* housing, being destroyed at an accelerating speed, Shanghai people's particular life style that commits to the nuances of all aspects of life vanishes with the demolition of the old alley houses. The overwhelming global sublime as shown by Pudong has to be seen side by side with urban changes such as the influx of illegal migrant workers, the demolition of alley housing, the involuntary relocation of residences, work-units, or factories. Wang's commitment to accumulating details of urban life to create the image of Shanghai glory on her own shows the contradiction entailed by the global city formation, the expansion of the conceived space for capital flows and the subjugated lived space of people's daily life. Yet, fundamentally, Wang's own image-making undertaking fails to problematize the production of the global city.

Coda

The past two decades of the twentieth century saw technological advances in communication and transportation facilitate capital globalization, which gives rise to a popular belief in a new global space that is fluid, flexible, and open to everyone democratically. Examining the validity of such a conception of space, I turn to Asian global cities such as Hong Kong, Tokyo, and Shanghai, whose urban geography has been radically reshaped to cater to the needs of flexible accumulation at an unprecedented speed. The social/historical account of the urban development of these cities during the campaign of their "global city formation" reveals how the idea of an infinite space opened up by global flows is mediated in development slogans, government white papers, or commercial films for real estate agency. Hong Kong people, Tokyoites and Shanghainese are instructed to make room for their metropolises to accelerate capital flows as well as to take pride in being a member of the global city, which supposedly should lead them to a prosperous utopia of possibilities. Pointing to the azure, the glittering skyscrapers become the sites where urbanites project their desire for a space of limitless aspirations despite the fact that many of them never get to use the monumental space in their everyday life. The collective longing for an open space enabled by globalization often finds its anchor in the monumental buildings in the city.

To address the question of whether the utopian aspect of globalization should also be represented and if one has to be completely pessimistic about the future of people's ability to be in control of their everyday life in the global city, I argue that the tone of this project on globalization is "critical" rather than "pessimistic." As I illustrated in these chapters, interest groups like nation-states, transnational corporations, real estate companies, multilateral financial organizations, and a small group of elite urban planners and architects have been disseminating and promulgating globalization as a decentralized, open space for everyone in every corner of the world. I choose to leave the happy story for them to tell. Yet, in the future when government officials or urban planners proudly present their campaign of global city formation and monumental buildings, hopefully they also have in mind the September 11 attacks and the needs of the exploited people before telling the grand narrative of globalization.

The artistic account in each chapter tells the story of walking in these global cities as an experience of oscillating between yearning and frustration. It is through the representation of walking in the films and novels that we see the contradictions inherent in the lingering belief in the open space mobilized by global flows. The walkers' footsteps compose "little narratives" of the concrete here-and-now of the global city as experienced rather than conceived by the individuals. The sense of melancholy, angst, and nostalgia these walkers display while wandering the streets of their cities suggests the fallacy of globalization as an immediate utopia without any inhibitions. Investigating the representation of walking in global cities, I conduct an inquiry into the way in which the power of capital, by re-inscribing the ideology of open space on the urban landscape, conceals or misrepresents the forbidden, confined, or monitored in the global city. The critique of the ideology of open space, presented through the politics of walking and the gap between the official account and the private account of the Asian global cities, is to provide a counter narrative to the myth of globalization as a progress to the best interest of all.

Bibliography

Abbas, Ackbar. *Hong Kong: Culture and the Politics of Disappearance*. Minneapolis: University of Minnesota Press, 1997.

——. "Cosmopolitan De-scriptions: Shanghai and Hong Kong." *Public Culture* 12.3 (2000): 769–86.

Appadurai, Arjun. *Modernity at Large: Cultural Dimensions of Globalization*. Minneapolis: U of Minnesota Press, 1996.

Appadurai, Arjun, and James Holston. "Cities and Citizenship." *Public Culture* 8.2 (1996): 187–204.

Bailey, Cameron. "Wong Kar-Wai's Works Show Enormous Energy." http://www.xs4all.nl/~chinaman (July 6, 1997).

Benjamin, Walter. "On Some Motifs in Baudelaire." *Illuminations*. Ed. Hannah Arendt. Trans. Harry Zohn. New York: Schocken Books, 1969. 155–200.

——. "The *Flâneur*." *Charles Baudelaire: A Lyric Poet in the Era of High Capitalism*. Trans. Harry Zohn. London: New Left Books, 1973. 35–66.

Bhabha, Homi, "Of Mimicry and Man: The Ambivalence of Colonial Discourse." Michelson et al. 125–33.

Borja, Jordi, and Manuel Castells. *Local and Global: The Management of Cities in the Information Age*. London: Earthscan, 1997.

Brenner, Robert. "The Economics of Global Turbulence." *New Left Review* 229 (1998): 1–265.

Bridge, Gary. "Mapping the Terrain of Time — Space Compression: Power Networks in Everyday Life." *Environment and Planning D: Society and Space* 15 (1997): 611–26.

Buckley, Roger. *Hong Kong: the Road to 1997*. New York: Cambridge UP, 1997.

Buck-Morss, Susan. "The *Flâneur*, the Sandwichman and the Whore: The Politics of Loitering." *New German Critique* 39 (1986): 99–140.

———. *The Dialectics of Seeing: Studies in Contemporary German Social Thought.* Cambridge: MIT Press, 1989.

Butler, Judith. *The Psychic Life of Power: Theories in Subjection.* Stanford: Stanford UP, 1997.

Caillois, Roger. "Mimicry and Legendary Psychasthenia." Trans. John Shepley. Michelson et al. 59–74.

Chan, Roger C. K. "Urban Development and Redevelopment." Yeung and Sung. 299–320.

Chen, Qingbai and Shi Wei. "Reestablishing Shanghai as an International Financial Center." *Beijing Review* 15–21 August 1994: 14–7.

Chen, Shaoneng. Ed. *The World-famous Multinational Corporations in Pudong, Shanghai.* Shanghai: East China Normal University Press, 1995.

Cheung, Peter T. Y. "The Political Context of Shanghai Economic Development." Yeung and Sung. 49–92.

Chiao, Hsiung-ping. "The Distinct Taiwanese and Hong Kong Cinemas." *Perspectives on Chinese Cinema.* Ed. Chris Berry. London: British Film Institute, 1991. 155–65.

Chow, Rey. "Things, Common/Places, Passages of the Port City: On Hong Kong and Hong Kong Author Leung Ping-kwan." *differences* 5 (1993): 179–204.

———. *Ethics After Idealism: Theory-Culture-Ethnicity-Reading.* Bloomington: Indiana UP, 1998.

Chu, Yiu-wai. *Bentu shenhua: quanqiuhua niandai de lunshu shengchan (Myth-making of the Local: The Production of Discourse in the Age of Globalization).* Taipei: Student Book, 2002.

Chungking Express. Dir. Kar-wai Wong. Scholar, 1993.

Ciment, Michael. "A Chat with Wong Kar-wai." *Positif* 410 (1995), http://www.xs4all.nl/~chinaman/chat.html#begin (July 6, 1997).

"City of the Plain." *The Economist* 18 March 1995: 18–9.

Coaldrake, Willam H. *Architecture and Authority in Japan.* New York: Routledge, 1996.

Cuthbert, Alexander. "Hong Kong 1997: The Transition to Socialism — Ideology, Discourse and Urban Spatial Structure." *Environment and Planning D: Society and Space* 5 (1987): 123–50.

———. "Under the Volcano: Postmodern Space in Hong Kong." Watson and Gibson. 138–48.

Cybriwsky, Roman. *Tokyo: The Shogun's City at the Twenty-First Century.* New York: John Wiley & Sons, 1998.

de Certeau, Michel. *The Practice of Everyday Life.* Trans. Steven Rendall. Berkeley: U of California Press, 1984.

Donald, James. "Metropolis: the City as Text." *Social and Cultural Forms of Modernity.* Eds. Robert Bocock and Kenneth Thompson. Cambridge: Polity, 1992. 417–70.

Fei, Xiaotong. "Turning Shanghai Into a 'Mainland Hong Kong.'" *Beijing Review* 22–28 October 1990: 25–7.

Gaubatz, Piper. "China's Urban Transformation: Patterns and Processes of Morphological Change in Beijing, Shanghai and Guangzhou." *Urban Studies* 36: 9 (August 1999): 1495–521.

Girard, René. *The Scapegoat*. Trans. Yvonne Freccero. Baltimore: Johns Hopkins UP, 1986.

Gleber, Anke. "Women on the Screen and Streets of Modernity: In Search of the Female *Flâneur*." *The Image in Dispute: Art and Cinema in the Age of Photography*. Ed. Dudley Andrew. U of Texas P, 1997. 55–85.

Gold, Thomas. "Can Pudong Deliver? Shanghai's Ambitious Planners Are Counting on Foreign Investors to Propel the New Development Area." *The China Business Review* November-December 1991: 22–9.

Gregory, Derek. *Geographical Imaginations*. Cambridge: Blackwell, 1994.

Guo, Bo. *Zhengzai xiaoshi de Shanghai longtang (Shanghai Longtang Houses on the Verge of Disappearing)*. Shanghai: Shanghai huabao chubanshe, 1996.

Harvey, David. *The Condition of Postmodernity: An Enquiry into the Origins of Cultural Change*. Cambridge: Blackwell, 1990.

———. *Spaces of Hope*. Berkeley: U of California Press, 2000.

Hill, Richard Child, and June Woo Kim. "Global Cities and Developmental States: New York, Tokyo and Seoul." *Urban Studies* 37.12 (2000): 2167–95.

Huang, Guoxin. Ed. *Kuashiji de Shanghai xinjianzhu (New and Trans-century Architecture in Shanghai)*, Volume III. Shanghai: Tonji daxue chubanshe, 2000.

Huus, Kari. "Boom and Busted: Shanghai construction takes off, but profits may fizzle." *Far Eastern Economic Review* 13 April 1995: 48–9.

Jacka, Tamara. "Wanted: Job for the Unwanted Migrant." http://www.chinaonline.com/commentary_analysis/economics/NewsArchive/Secure/2000/December (December 4, 2000).

Jameson, Fredric. *The Geopolitical Aesthetic: Cinema and Space in the World System*. Bloomington, Indiana UP, 1992.

Kang, Yan. *Jiedu Shanghai: 1990 to 2000 (Understanding Shanghai: From 1990 to 2000)*. Shanghai: Shanghai renmin chubanshe, 2001.

King, Anthony D. *Global Cities: Post-Imperialism and the Internationalization of London*. New York: Routledge, 1990.

Kwan, Chi Hung. "The Plight of the Hong Kong Economy — SARS is not the only culprit." http://www.rieti.go.jp/en/index.html (May 23, 2003).

Lai, Lawrence W. C. "The Property Price Crisis." *The Other Hong Kong Report 1994*. Eds. Donald H. McMillen and Si-Wai Man. Hong Kong: Chinese UP, 1994. 187–208.

Lammie, David. "Pudong Development Zone." *Contemporary Review* 262 (1993): 174–77.

Landler, Mark. "Hong Kong Is Hoping Disney Magic Rubs Off." *New York Times*. 21 November 1999: TR 3.
Lau, Chi Kuen. *Hong Kong's Colonial Legacy*. Hong Kong: Chinese UP, 1997.
Law, Lisa. "Defying Disappearance: Cosmopolitan Public Spaces in Hong Kong." *Urban Studies* 39.6 (2002): 1625–45.
Lefebvre, Henri. *The Production of Space*. Trans. Donald Nicholson-Smith. Oxford: Basil Blackwell, 1974.
Leung, P. K. "The Sorrows of Lan Kwai Fong." *Hong Kong Collage: Contemporary Stories and Writing*. Ed. Martha P. Y. Cheung. New York: Oxford UP, 1998. 85–95.
Li, Ning. "Global Top 500 To Meet in Shanghai." *Beijing Review* 20 September 1999: 12–5.
Li, Peilin. Ed. *Zhong guo shinshiqi jieji jieceng baogao (Transition in Social Stratification in the Market China)*. Shenyang: Liaoning renmin chubanshe, 1995.
Liao, Ye. "Shanghai Economy On Fast Track." *Beijing Review* 7–13 March 1994: 19–20.
"Life and Episodes in the Longtangs."
http://www.chinawindow.com/shanghai1/longtang/culture/fengqing.html.
Luo, Xiaowei and Wu Jiang. *Shanghai Longtang*. Shanghai: Shanghai renmin meishu chubanshe, 1997.
Maass, Harald. "Faster, Taller, More: Shanghai is Young and in a Hurry." *New World* 2 (2000): 16–23.
Machimura, Takashi. "The Urban Restructuring Process in Tokyo in the 1980s: Transforming Tokyo into a World City." *International Journal of Urban and Regional Research* 16.1 (1992): 114–28.
——. "Symbolic Use of Globalization in Urban Politics in Tokyo." *International Journal of Urban and Regional Research* 22. 2 (June 1998): 183–94.
Michelson, Annette, Rosalind Krauss, Douglas Crimp, and Joan Copjec eds. *October: The First Decade, 1976–1986*. Cambridge: MIT, 1987.
"Mimicry." *The New Encyclopedia Britannica*. 15th ed. 1998.
Morris, Jan. *Hong Kong: Epilogue to an Empire*. New York: Penguin, 1988.
Noyes, John K. *The Mastery of Submission: Inventions of Masochism*. Ithaca: Cornell UP, 1997.
Ogura, M. "Building Dearth in Tokyo." *Tokyo Business Today* August 1986: 16–24.
Olds, Kris. "Globalization and the Production of New Urban Spaces: Pacific Rim Megaprojects in the Late 20th Century." *Environment and Planning A* 27 (1995): 1713–43.
——. "Globalizing Shanghai: the 'Global Intelligence Corps' and the building of Pudong." *Cities* 14.2 (1997): 109–23.
Pile, Steve. *The Body and the City: Psychoanalysis, Space and Subjectivity*. London: Routledge, 1996.

Popham, Peter. *Tokyo: The City at the End of the World.* New York: Kodansha International P, 1985.

Rafferty, Kevin. *City on the Rocks: Hong Kong's Uncertain Future.* New York: Viking, 1989.

Said, Edward. "Islam and the West Are Inadequate Banners." *The Observer* 16 September 2000.

Sassen, Saskia. *The Global City: New York, London, Tokyo.* Princeton: Princeton UP, 1991.

——. "Whose City Is It? Globalization and the Formation of New Claims." *Public Culture* 8.2 (1996): 205–23.

——. "Swirling That Old Wine Around in the Wrong Bottle: A Comment on White." *Urban Affairs Review* 33.4 (1998a): 478–81.

——. *Globalization and Its Discontents: Essays on the New Mobility of People and Money.* New York: New P, 1998b.

Segal, Gerald. *The Fate of Hong Kong.* New York: St. Martin's Press, 1993.

"Shanghai Financial Center: Challenging the New Height." *Min Sheng Daily* 2 October 2001: A12.

"Shanghai Mayor on Pudong Development." *Beijing Review* 24–30 September 1990: 23–6.

"Shanghai Takes Shape." *The Economist* 3 May 1997: 27–8.

Shen, Qing. "Urban Transportation in Shanghai, China: Problems and Planning Implications." *International Journal of Urban and Regional Research* 21.4 (December 1997): 589–606.

Shields, Rob. *Lefebvre, Love & Struggle: Spatial Dialectics.* New York: Routledge, 1999.

Simmel, Georg. "The Metropolis and Mental Life." *The Sociology of Georg Simmel.* Trans. Kurt H. Wolff. Illinois: Free Press, 1950. 409–24.

Skeldon, Ronald. "Immigration and Population Issues." *The Other Hong Kong Report 1995.* Eds. Stephen Y. L. Cheung and Stephen M. H. Sze. Hong Kong: Chinese UP, 1995. 303–16.

——. "Labour Market Developments and Foreign Worker Policy in Hong Kong." *Migration and the Labour Market in Asia: Prospects to the Year 2000.* Paris: OECD, 1996. 183–94

Smart, Alan. *Making Room: Squatter Clearance in Hong Kong.* Hong Kong: Centre of Asian Studies, 1992.

Solnit, Rebecca. *Wanderlust: A History of Walking.* New York: Penguin Putnam, 2000.

"Speech by Jiang Zemin at the Banquet to Celebrate the Opening of the '99 Fortune Global Forum in Shanghai." *Beijing Review* 18 October 1999: 8–9.

Stallybrass, Peter, and Allon White. *The Politics & Poetics of Transgression.* Ithaca: Cornell UP, 1986.

Stephens, Chuck. "Time Pieces: Wong Kar-wai and the Persistence of Memory." *Film Comment.* January 1996, 12–8.

Stokes, Lisa Odham, and Michael Hoover. *City on Fire: Hong Kong Cinema*. New York: Verso, 1999.
Streshinsky, Shirley. "Shanghai Sees the Light." *Preservation* September/October (2000): 34–82.
Sun, Haiming and Liu Naichuan. "First-Class World Cities and the Urbanization of Pudong." Yao et al. 133–47.
Tajima, Noriyuki. *Tokyo: A Guide to Recent Architecture*. London: Ellipsis London Limited, 1995.
Tang, James T. H. "Hong Kong in Transition: Globalization Versus Nationalization." *The Challenge of Hong Kong's Reintegration with China*. Ed. Ming K. Chan. Hong Kong: Hong Kong UP, 1997. 177–97.
Tasker, Peter. *Inside Japan: Wealth, Work and Power in the New Japanese Empire*. London: Sidgwick & Jackson, 1987.
Tester, Keith. Ed. *The Flâneur*. New York: Routledge, 1994.
Tetsuo: The Iron Man. Dir. Shinya Tsukamoto. Kaijyu Theatre, 1989.
Tetsuo II: Body Hammer. Dir. Shinya Tsukamoto. Kaijyu Theatre, 1992.
Tokyo Fist. Dir. Shinya Tsukamoto. Kaijyu Theatre, 1995.
Tokyo Metropolitan Government. *2nd Long-term Plan for the Tokyo Metropolis*. Tokyo: Tokyo Metropolitan Government P, 1987.
——. *Tokyo: Yesterday, Today and Tomorrow*. Tokyo: Tokyo Metropolitan Government P, 1989.
Tsukamoto, Shinya. Interview. *Alles: Internet Voice Magazine*. http://www.express.co.jp/alles/2/tsukamoto1.html
Udagawa, Hideo. "Tokyo Reaches the Outer Limits." *Tokyo Business Today* April 1988: 34–7.
Vogel, Ezra F. *Japan as Number One: Lessons for America*. Cambridge: Harvard UP, 1979.
Walden, John. "Calendar of Events in 1996–1997." *The Other Hong Kong Report 1997*. Ed. Joseph Y.S. Cheng. Hong Kong: Chinese UP, 1997. vii–xxix.
Wang, Anyi. *Changhenge (The Song of Unending Sorrow)*. Taipei: Rye Field Press, 2000.
——. *Meitou (Sister)*. Taipei: Rye Field Press, 2001.
Wang, Xiaoming and Li Tuo. Eds. *Zai shinyishixingtai de longzhaoxia: jiuling niandai de wenhua he wenxue fenxi (Under the Influence of a New Ideology: Analysis of Chinese Culture and Literature of the 1990s)*. Nanjing: Jiangsu renmin chubanshe, 1999.
Watson, Sophie and Katherine Gibson. Eds. *Postmodern Cities and Spaces*. Cambridge: Blackwell, 1995.
Weinstein, Deena, and Michael A. Weinstein. *Postmodern(ized) Simmel*. New York: Routledge, 1993.
Welsh, Frank. *A Borrowed Place: the History of Hong Kong*. New York: Kodansha, 1993.

Wilcox, Joe. "IBM to Spend $300 Million on Shanghai Chip Plant." http://www.nytimes.com/cnet/CNET-0-4-3304666-00.html (October 26, 2000).

Wilson, Elizabeth. "The Invisible *Flâneur.*" Watson and Gibson. 59–79.

Wolf, Jaime. "The Occidental Tourist." http://www.xs4all.nl/~chinaman/chat.html#begin (July 6, 1997).

Wolff, Janet. "The Invisible *Flâneuse*: Women and the Literature of Modernity." *Theory, Culture and Society* 2.3 (1985): 37–48.

Wong, Hung. "Marginalization Crisis of Hong Kong Labour: The Impact of Economic Reunification of China and Hong Kong." *Hong Kong SAR: In Pursuit of Domestic and International Order.* Eds. Beatrice Leung and Joseph Cheng. Hong Kong: Chinese UP, 1997. 73–96.

Wood, Christopher. *The Bubble Economy: Japan's Extraordinary Speculative Boom of the '80s and the Dramatic Bust of the '90s.* New York: Atlantic Monthly P, 1992.

Wu, Fulong. "The Global and Local Dimensions of Place-making: Remaking Shanghai as a World City." *Urban Studies* 37.8 (2000): 1359–77.

Xin, Zhou. "Shanghai at Night." *Beijing Review* 4–10 August 1997: 16–9.

Yahuda, Michael. *Hong Kong: China's Challenge.* New York: Routledge, 1996.

Yao, Xitang et al. *Yongpan fengdian: Pudong kaifa kaifang shinian fazhan yanjiu chengguo jicui (Challenging the New Height: A Decade of Development of Pudong, Shanghai).* Shanghai: Shanghai Academy of Social Sciences, 2000.

Yatsko, Pamela. "Field of Dreams: Can Shanghai re-emerge as a key financial centre? " *Far Eastern Economic Review* 18 July 1996a: 69–70.

——. "Future Shock: Shanghai remakes itself as workers search for a role." *Far Eastern Economic Review* 29 August 1996b: 58–9.

Yeh, Anthony G. O. "Pudong—the Remaking of Shanghai as a World City" in Yeung and Sung. 274–97.

Yeh, Yueh-yu. "A Life of Its Own: Musical Discourses in Wong Kar-wai's Films." *Phantom of the Music: Song Narration and Chinese-language Cinema.* Taipei: Yuan-Liou, 2000. 123–54.

Yeung, Yue-man. *Globalization and Networked Societies: Urban-Regional Change in Pacific Asia.* Honolulu: U of Hawaii P, 2000.

Yeung, Y. M. and Y. W. Sung. Eds. *Shanghai: Transformation and Modernization Under China's Open Door Policy.* Hong Kong: Chinese University of Hong Kong, 1996.

Notes

INTRODUCTION

1 As Edward Said argues, Islam and the West are inadequate banners to comprehend the attacks.
2 Such a tendency to abstract the bodily experience and deprive the space of the body is what Derek Gregory calls the violence of abstract space, that of decorporealization. A good scenario to demonstrate decorporealization can be as follows: an investment broker steps into an office building to monitor through telecommunications global capital flows. The object of the gaze turns to be what is seen through the technological eyes, for instance, the figures of a foreign stock market on a computer screen. To see with the eyes of the machine seduces one to elide the immediate surroundings. A perfect world defined by the rule of time-space compression allows little space for corporeality.
3 I would hasten to add, my argument prioritizes the physical sense of walking over the metaphorical one since such a seemingly simple physical act enables the city-users to experience the urban space of everyday life, and thus serves as a powerful vehicle to examine the widely disseminated belief in the open space of globalization from a micro-level. Representing urbanites' walking and seeing in the global city, I hope to lay bare the paradoxes of life in contemporary global cities. The glamorous cityscape that the eye sees all the time (e.g. the monumental buildings) often contradicts what the body experiences on a daily basis (e.g. living in a small apartment in a high-rise project).
4 She identifies the huge population of low-income Others as "African Americans, immigrants, and women" (1996: 221). Sassen explains the two expanding classes in the global city are the "top-level professional workers largely in the corporate sector" and "the other types of economic activities and workers" (1998a: 480).
5 The title of Bill Clinton's speech in Taipei is "Our Shared Future: Globalization in

the 21st Century." Clinton's trip to Asia (scheduled to arrive in Taiwan on September 12) was cancelled because of the terrorists' attacks in New York City and Washington D.C.

6 As Rob Shields summarizes, "[a] large portion of *Production of Space* is devoted to developing a radical phenomenology of space as a humanistic basis from which to launch a critique of the denial of individual and community's 'right to space' under the abstract spatialisation embodied in capitalism and technocratic knowledge structures of the state" (146).

7 For a historical account of the theorization of the global city, see Hill and Kim "Global Cities and Developmental States." As Hill and Kim point out, while Friedmann and King use the term "world city," Sassen prefers "the global city" (2188). In contemporary theories of globalization, it is not unusual to see the terms "world city," "global city," and "command-post city" used interchangeably.

8 The reason why I exclude Beijing, Seoul, or Taipei is not that they are fundamentally different from Hong Kong, Tokyo and Shanghai as global cities, but rather the latter three are better representatives of global cities in degree.

9 While following Lefebvre's theorization of space to divide discourses into the official and the private, I do not intend to imply a clear-cut separation between the official space and the private space. On the contrary, my juxtaposition of the official account and the private account of the global cities seeks to emphasize the complexity between the public and the private life in the metropolises. To be precise, the theoretical framework is more the official account versus the private account of the global city (representation of space and representational space in Lefebvre's words) rather than official space against private space. The divergence and convergence of these two accounts reveal how the global space of the city subjugates and compresses the living space of everyday life. The Lefebvrian method effectively helps us identify that the official narrative of a global city and the private account of the same urban space could be enmeshed together, and the international mobility of global capital is tightly related to the mobility of the urban inhabitants.

10 I use the term "global flows" to describe global capital accumulation in relation to globalization. As Saskia Sassen and David Harvey argue, one distinctive feature of globalization is the unprecedented deterritorialized circulation of capital due to liberalization of the market and the accelerating turnover time of capital, made possible by technological development. Grasping the process of globalization in terms of "flows" helps to reveal the often veiled operations of such transnational financial agglomeration. Urban geographer Kris Olds also uses such terms as "cross-border capital flows" and "financial flows" to explain specific aspects of the restructuring of global financial systems (1995: 1715).

11 Harvey defines the concept of time-space compression as "processes that so revolutionize the objective qualities of space and time that we are forced to

alter, sometimes in quite radical ways, how we represent the world to ourselves" (1990: 240). The distinctive difference between modernism and postmodernism exactly lies in our new perception of space and time: "[w]e have been experiencing, these last two decades, an intense phase of time-space compression that has had a disorienting and disruptive impact upon political — economic practices, the balance of class power, as well as upon cultural and social life" (1990: 284).

CHAPTER 1

1 From a British colony to socialist China's Special Administrative Region after the handover in 1997, Hong Kong's postcoloniality has received much attention and discussion because of its unique history. It is important to note that Hong Kong's postcoloniality cannot be disentangled from capital globalization. As Yiuwai Chu points out, Hong Kong's postcoloniality has to be situated not only in the context of global capitalism but also in the space of the metropolis (129, 172). In other words, Hong Kong as a global city functions as a strategic site to explore Hong Kong's postcolonial imagination.
2 Lantau Island is twice as big as Hong Kong Island. It is a resort for Hong Kong people when they need to take a break from the noisy city life, a "primitive" land where high-rise buildings or fancy recreational facilities are scarce.
3 Such a mechanism of global capital is what David Harvey defines as postmodernity.
4 Bridge points out Lefebvre's influence on Harvey. In fact, Harvey's "proposed schema for the translation of the global forces of capital accumulation and the individual experience of space and time utilises Lefebvre's (1991a) conception of the production of space through the interrelations between imagined, perceived, and experienced (or lived) space" (613).
5 Mike Rowse, Hong Kong's tourism commissioner, estimates that the theme park will bring in $19 billion over four decades, a fast turn-over profit, given its cost of US$3.6 billion.
6 The global compression, a force that demands an ever-expanding strategic space in the city for capital flows, drastically deprives the urban space of the old city users, in particular, those who have no access to the spatial forms of global space.
7 James T. H. Tang points out that according to the Heritage Foundation's *Index of Economic Freedom*, "[i]n recent years Hong Kong has been consistently ranked the most liberal economy in the world with virtually no barriers to trade and capital flow . . . " (177).
8 Suzie Wong, the prostitute in the novel *The World of Suzie Wong*, lived in the Luk Kwok Hotel, which was demolished for new urban development (Rafferty 60).

9 By "placeless" architecture, Abbas means those hotels and office buildings with no local memories (1997: 82).
10 Wanchai is the chosen site for entrepreneur Gordon Wu's 90-story high hotel, a plan announced before Hong Kong's tallest building, Bank of China Tower, opened in 1989 (Rafferty 57).
11 For a detailed physical description of the two buildings, see Abbas, 1997: 84–5.
12 The bank claims it cost HK$5 billion, but this estimate does not include the cost of the land (owned by the bank itself) and the high furnishing cost. One staff member's remarks, a typical view of the fancy building, show how monumentality shapes a collective will to power. Asked about the incredible cost of the building, the staff member says, "[w]e have a fine building. What does it cost? — a few years' profits, but it's put us on the world architectural map" (Rafferty 294).
13 The exhibit was promoted by the Hong Kong Institute of Professional Photographers to raise funds for young photographers for advanced studies by public auction of photographs (Leung 93).
14 As Abbas notes, Lan Kwai Fong predominantly appeals to the affluent. Due to its high cost of admission, teenagers can sample the flavor of this trendy spot by strolling its streets, a pleasure not too different from "window shopping" (1997: 87).
15 Chek Lap Kok Airport is supposed to replace Kai Tak with its capacity of handling 35 million passengers and 1.5 million tons of cargo a year (Buckley 133).
16 The dowry metaphor implies a sexist ideology of the handover: Hong Kong is compared to a daughter to be married, with Britain her father, and China her husband. As Gayle Rubin points out, trafficking in women guarantees a patriarchal society its power and mastery.
17 "[E]very time relations between Britain and China become strained the future of the airport is threatened" (Welsh 534).
18 "When completed, it will be by far the most modern airport in China, and will act as the international gateway [for mainland China], thus fortifying the economic pre-eminence of Guangdong over the rest of the country" (Welsh 534).
19 "It was Japanese banks more than any other players who could make or break such major investment projects as the new airport in Hong Kong, but these decisions would be made on the basis of global trends in interest rates and rates of return on investment around the globe" (Segal 167).
20 Nathan Road, laid out between 1904 and 1907, is the major road that cuts through Kowloon, now the world famous "golden mile."
21 Among the Vietnamese migrants, those who came from China (ex-China Vietnamese illegal immigrants) are to be deported. Hong Kong government's increasingly high-handed policy toward Vietnamese migrants culminates in April 1994: "500 prisons officers, in full riot gear and with use of tear gas, make successful dawn swoop on the Whitehead Detention Centre and move 1,456 Vietnamese internees to High Island" (McMillen and Man xxi).

22 No sight in Hong Kong crystallizes the contradictory space of global city more clearly than Central on Sundays. Anyone who has paid a visit to Central on Sundays can hardly miss the quintessential scene of the dual city claimed by the global capitalists and the marginal people. Instead of the flow of well-groomed white-collar workers, the upscale Central on Sundays is occupied by thousands of Filipino maids, who gather in small groups at the open spaces among the skyscrapers in the hope of shaping a community in a foreign land. Jan Morris summarizes how these foreign laborers claim Central for their own use.

> Every Sunday morning, throughout the year, Statue Square is taken over by the Filipina maids of Hong Kong, who assemble here in their thousands to meet friends, swap news, cook al fresco meals, sell things to each other, read the Manila newspaper and sometimes dance to the music of transistors…. The women swarm upon the square in mid-morning [after their mass] pouring out of the subway stations, streaming off the ferries, and settling upon every bench, every patch of ground in a great eddy of shopping bags. If it is wet they occupy arcades, pedestrian bridges and shopping centres for half a mile around (104-5).

The Filipino maids make themselves visible actors that refuse to be overlooked by means of their festival Sunday gatherings at the very center of the city, surrounded by those glass buildings that signify capital and phallic power (the Statue Square is opposite to HSBC Headqaurters and adjacent to the fancy Mandarin Oriental Hotel). Yet their seemingly subversive claim to the urban glamour space cannot overlook the fact that these maids are foreign workers with low paid and few legal rights. For an insightful analysis of how foreign domestic laborers stake claims on Hong Kong's public space, see Lisa Law, "Defying Disappearance: Cosmopolitan Public Spaces in Hong Kong," *Urban Studies* 39.6 (2002), pp.1625–45.

23 Due to the large number of immigrants in the late 1970s and the consequent surplus of labor force, the Hong Kong government imposed a new immigration policy that requires legal documents for Mainland Chinese to work and stay in Hong Kong. It is not until the early 1990s, with new infrastructure projects to be completed, that a shortage of labor forced Hong Kong to open the door for importing laborers. For example, the project of a US$20 billion airport at Chek Lap Kok put forward the urgent need for construction workers. The scheme for the new airport allows 2,000 construction workers from China in 1990, 17,000 in 1994, and finally 27,000 in 1996 to help with the grand project. An important source of male labor is illegal immigration from China (Cuthbert 1995: 147).

24 Illegal immigrants from China to Hong Kong have been a concern for both parties. Before the handover, the Hong Kong police and the Chinese government

launched a large-scale anti-illegal-immigration campaign. About 2,000 policemen of Guangdong Province participated in the Shenzhen campaign to prevent a large number of illegal immigrants from taking advantage of the approaching handover. It was believed that Hong Kong SAR would cut a deal with illegal immigrants in Hong Kong after the sovereignty was transferred to China (Walden xxvi).

25 The expatriates from international corporations and the returned emigrated professionals, estimated at least 12% of the emigrated, also contribute to the problem of local concentration (Skeldon 1995: 311). Their usually luxurious and spacious living space is a sharp contrast to the overcrowded public housing. Their demand of the urban space, supported by the global capital influx, ensures the escalating price in the housing market and leaves half of the local population packed in the public housing.

26 Hong Kong, along with Singapore, has the world's largest public housing program, with 47% of its population living in such housing projects, and forty thousand new flats a year are built to meet the increasing demand (Borja and Castells 145).

27 As Abbas maintains, "[h]yperdensity is partly the result of limited space, but it is also a result of how this limited space could be exploited for economic gain" (1997: 86).

28 "Before the June 4 incident, Japanese companies were very active in the second-hand market but their leading position was taken over by Chinese enterprises after the event" (Lai 189).

29 The minimalist nature of Hong Kong's town planning indicates another strategy for the state to have the maximum flexibility of the land-use.

30 In the 1970s the formerly rural areas of the New Territories have undergone significant urbanization, and the agricultural way of life, which was still clearly discernible a quarter-century ago, has disappeared (Rafferty 84–9).

31 Residential densities average 7,000 persons per hectare (Cuthbert 1987: 144).

32 "On average a new housing unit is opened every 7.5 minutes of the working day" (Rafferty 20).

CHAPTER 2

1 By cognitive mapping, I follow Jameson's use of the term. As Colin MacCabe notes, for Jameson "cognitive mapping is a way of understanding how the individual's representation of his or her social world can escape the traditional critique of representation because the mapping is intimately related to practice—to the individual's successful negotiation of urban space" (xiv).

2 Quite a few critics have pointed out a striking resemblance between Brigitte Lin's character and Gena Roland's Gloria, a gangster in Cassavettes's film of the same title (Stokes and Hoover 197).

Notes to Pages 33–40   **153**

3   See Andre Breton's film *Nadja*.
4   The airport in the film is the former international airport, Kai Tak (1925–1998).
5   For detailed discussion of the dynamics between Hong Kong's phenomenal economic success and its cultural space, see Rey Chow's "Things, Common/Places, Passages of the Port City: On Hong Kong and Hong Kong Author Leung Ping-kwan" and Ackbar Abbas's *Hong Kong: Culture and the Politics of Disappearance*, chapter 1.
6   Wong describes her walk in Chungking Mansion as "an animal roving" in the jungle (http://www.wongkarwai.net/stories.php?story=01/05/04/7440916).
7   For a comprehensive analysis of the dynamics between the idea of pollution and the division of urban space as well as the resonance between bodies and cities, see Stallybrass and White, *The Politics & Poetics of Transgression*.
8   For example, Arjun Appadurai argues that cities tend to replace nations as the social imaginary of citizenship and to represent the localization of global forces. See "Cities and Citizenship."
9   "Love at last sight" is quoted from Baudelaire's famous sonnet "Á une passante," in which the poet is fascinated by a woman passing by in the street and doomed to miss his object of desire forever after that fleeting chance encounter. Benjamin argues that "the delight of the urban poet is love—not at first sight, but at last sight. It is a farewell forever which coincides in the poem with the moment of enchantment" (1969: 169).
10 Elizabeth Wilson argues that city as a labyrinth designates the decline of masculine power. She believes that "[v]oyeurism and commodification lead to the attenuation and deferral of satisfaction" (74). The Baudelairean spleen indeed results from male impotence. Walking in the city is one of the activities that fight against the destructive spleen. See "The Invisible *Flâneur*."
11 As Alexander Cuthbert points out, there have been two dominant discourses in Hong Kong — traditional Chinese Confucianism-Taoism and British colonialism. A third discursive system, the socialism of People's Republic of China, becomes more and more influential because of the handover. In other words, "Hong Kong is crossing an ideological tightrope from the discourse of capitalism to that of socialism" (1995: 145).
12 According to Benjamin, shock experience is closely related to the encounter with the metropolitan crowds in the fragmentary urban life. He quotes Freud to explain shock:

> For a living organism, protection against stimuli is an almost more important function than the reception of stimuli; the protective shield is equipped with its own store of energy and must above all strive to preserve the special forms of conversion of energy operating in it against the effects . . . which tend toward an equalization of potential and hence toward destruction. (1969: 161)

Benjamin thus argues, "[t]he threat from these energies is one of shocks. The more readily consciousness registers these shocks, the less likely are they to have a traumatic effect" (1969: 161).

13 According to Freud, "melancholia is the effect of unavowable loss" (Butler 170).
14 OK convenience store is a transnational franchised business in East Asia.
15 223's password to his voicemail system, "love you 10,000 years," speaks for his desire for a less mutable space.
16 Lisa Stokes and Michael Hoover consider this change as one of the many changes that requires explanation in the film: how does 633 afford purchasing the fast-food counter? (196) Yet his taking over Midnight Express from the owner, who newly opens a Karaoke bar, can also be regarded as a realistic example of Hong Kong's fast-changing space.
17 Working at Midnight Express, Faye seems to be confined by the limited space of the fast food stand, separated from the crowd by the counter. Yet from the very beginning Faye destabilizes her image as a woman circumscribed by space with her improvised dancing at work. Dancing to her favorite song "California Dreamin'," with pots and pans in hands, Faye somehow manages to liberate herself from the claustrophobic and monotonous space of Midnight Express.
18 As Anke Gleber notes, "[l]imited excursions of shopping in a prescribed ghetto of consumption amount to little more than secondhand distraction, never approximating the flaneur's wide-reaching mode of perception, unimpeded by aims, purposes, and schedules" (59–60).
19 The ideology of inviting global flows lingers even after China's takeover: after France, Hong Kong will join the Disneyland franchise soon after the millennium.

CHAPTER 3

1 Benjamin's study of Paris arcades is an effort to historicize "[p]laces that were incomprehensible yesterday, and that tomorrow will never know" (qtd. in Abbas 1997: 8).
2 Cameron Bailey, "Wong Kar-Wai's Works Show Enormous Energy," http://www.xs4all.nl/~chinaman, 6 July 1997.
3 Michael Ciment, "A Chat with Wong Kar-wai," *Positif* 410 (1995), http://www.xs4all.nl/~chinaman/chat.html#begin, 6 July 1997.
4 Jaime Wolf, "The Occidental Tourist, " http://www.xs4all.nl/~chinaman/chat.html#begin, 6 July 1997.
5 Benjamin describes *flâneur* as such: "His leisurely appearance as a personality is his protest against the division of labour which makes people into specialists" (1973: 54).
6 Film critic Chiao Hsiung-Ping argues that "[t]he only special characteristics of Hong Kong cinema are precisely entertainment and commerce" (159). Chuck

Stephens comments on Wong's role in Hong Kong's film industry as such: "Prone to musings on stylists as varied as John Ford and Manuel Puig, Haruki Murakami and Alain Renais, Wong's films are as distinctly representative of the myriad flavors and cultural influences that comprise cosmopolitan Hong Kong as they are disparate from the mainstream that he has at last begun to influence" (3).

7 The overlapping part of the representation of space and the representational space, for instance, the congested, hybrid, compartmentalized urban space, is addressed in the early discussion of specific walkers and their journeys in the film.

8 The yearning for taking a less-trodden path echoes that of the romantic poets, who envision themselves as solitary bards wandering the world.

9 In a sense, the image of overcrowded high-rise public housing is represented through Chungking Mansion and Cop 633's apartment. The sense of a congested and compartmentalized space one identifies in these two spaces more or less parallels the lived space in public housing. One way to account for the invisible public housing in the film is the "logic of the place" Wong endeavors to follow. For example, Faye's improvised walk from where she works to 633's place is hardly imaginable if 633 lives at a high-rise housing project at distant New Territories instead of an apartment in the same area Central. Wong opts for Chungking Mansion rather than any anonymous residential building also lies in the fact that Chungking Mansion is a building of local memories, both personal and collective — another example of the director-*flâneur's* resistance to globalization. The desire to register Chungking Mansion as the authentic local renders the multi-ethnic and multinational space of the building a site of mystery. For example, a walk in Chungking Mansion brings to light how the compartmentalized space of the building is monitored. Next to the elevators are the video cameras showing the interior of each elevator. The director-*flâneur* shoots the woman in the blonde wig taking the elevator to meet the Indians, yet the technological apparatus of surveillance remains out of sight.

10 Like the blonde-wigged woman walker in his film, Wong always wears sunglasses in public.

11 On July 1, 2003, more than 500,000 Hong Kong people demonstrated against the proposed internal-security bill known as Article 23 of the Basic Law in the hope of sustaining freedom and democracy for their city. Looking back at Hong Kong today, six years after the handover and a few weeks after the SARS outbreak was officially over, I find it necessary to update my descriptions of Hong Kong as a dream land of capital and democracy.

Obviously the virus flow of the global city severely impedes the capital flow. However, it is worth noting that just as Tokyo witnessed a decade's economic decline after Japan's bubble burst in the 1990s, Hong Kong has suffered two recessions since 1997. Evidence of the lackluster economy since Asia's financial crises of 1997 abounds: sluggish property market, fallback in trading volumes, and high unemployment rate, just to name a few. As Chi Hung Kwan points out,

> Average annual economic growth in the five years since reversion has been about 2.5 percent — a far cry from the 5 percent that was seen in the five years prior to 1997. Conversely, unemployment, which stood at 2.2 percent in 1997, has surged to currently stand at 7.5 percent. In addition to a series of external shocks such as the 1997-8 Asian financial crisis and SARS, the Hong Kong economy is being further hit by the decline of its predominance in intermediating China's international trade.

To be precise, in addition to the SARS Epidemic and Asia's financial crisis, Hong Kong's economic slowdown can also be attributed to the strong intervention from China, beleaguered global economy in recent years, and keen competition with rival cities such as Singapore, Shenzhen and Shanghai.

From the world's top financial center to a city threatened by serious economic setbacks and mounting political crisis, changes in Hong Kong once again seem to validate Abbas's description of the city as "a space of disappearance." Yet I hasten to add that the relationship between the economic downturn of the global city and the city users' imaginary and material claims to the urban space requires further rigorous research.

12 For example, residents of Lantau Island must live with a US$20 billion airport and a Disney theme park.

13 Other filmic elements that suggest the omnipresent globalization in Hong Kong include the music, particularly the theme song of Faye's story, "California Dreamin'," which implies Faye's global dream as well as her walk as sleepwalking. The scenes where Faye runs into 633 in the local street market also illuminate the presence of global space. Against the background music of Cantonese opera and the image of a traditional market, Faye confides in her dream of going to California. For a detailed analysis of the music in Wong Kar-wai's films, see Yeh Yueh-yu's "A Life of Its Own: Musical Discourses in Wong Kar-wai's Films" in *Phantom of the Music: Song Narration and Chinese-language Cinema*.

14 Again, Benjamin's metaphor of phantasmagoria helps to grasp how globalization and its ideology of economic success reshape Hong Kong's cultural/urban landscape. Derek Gregory's explication of why Benjamin uses the phantasmagoria to allegorize modern culture explicates the analogy drawn here:

> [p]ainted slides were illuminated in such a way that a succession of ghosts ("phantasms") was paraded before a startled audience. But the phantasmagoria was no ordinary lantern, because it used back-projection to ensure that the audience remained largely unaware of the source of the image: Its flickering creations

thus appeared to be endowed "with a spectral reality of their own." (231–3)

PART TWO

1 For the social tension resulted from the expansion of business space in central Tokyo, see Machimura 126-7. For examples of resistance to the urban rezoning, see Peter Popham's *Tokyo: the City at the End of the World*, Chapter 3.
2 1,770 apartments are being built at the east side of the river (Tajima 88).
3 Indeed, Ohkawabashi River City 21 can be seen as a textbook case of Lefebvre's theory of metonymy and metaphor. See Lefebvre 96–9.

CHAPTER 4

1 In a sense, Lefebvre reads against Plato's endorsement of mimesis as a necessary instrument to nurture the guardian class.
2 As Takashi Machimura points out, "in the 1980s, when Japan experienced trade disputes with the United States and the EC, the rapid up-valuation of the yen and financial globalization, Japanese capital began to transnationalize on a greater scale" (1992: 116). For a discussion of bubble economy and the trade disputes with the US, see the first chapter of Christopher Wood's *Bubble Economy* and *New Left Review* 229 (1998), 231–36. From 1981 to 1984 about 30,000 domestic companies moved their head offices to Tokyo and in 1985 the total number of companies in Tokyo reached 390,000. Foreign companies also poured into Tokyo; 1985 alone saw about 100 finance and securities companies settling down in the city. For example, IBM moved its Far Eastern headquarters from Hong Kong to Tokyo in 1985 with an astonishing acquisition of 100,000 meter-square of office space (Ogura 19).
3 For a detailed discussion of the relationships between the company and the salaryman, see Ezra F. Vogel's *Japan as Number One: Lessons for America*, 131-57 and Peter Tasker's *Inside Japan: Wealth, Work and Power in the New Japanese Empire*, 87–99.
4 The large floor space of 400,000 square meters accommodates 13,000 employees. Upon its completion in 1991, the official cost of the buildings is US$ 1.23 billion (160 billion yen) (Tajima 220).
5 The New City Hall embodies what Lefebvre calls "an ideology in action" (308).
6 For a detailed discussion of the analogy between the Edo castle and the New City Hall, see William Coaldrake's *Architecture and Authority*.
7 The architectural details of the New City Hall complex also function to boost the civic consciousness. They convey a strong sense of practicality, of serving the city-users literally from a pedestrian level. The pedestrian access to the city hall was promoted as an indispensable part of the package of the construction of

the sublime towers. In so doing, Shinjuku subcenter is expected to transform into a comfortable environment for the walkers (Tokyo Metropolitan Government 1989: 74). Another pertinent example can be found in the "Citizens' Plaza," located between the assembly building and the No. 1 building. The semi-oval plaza, reminiscent of Vatican's St. Peter's Square, was designed to "create a symbolic space serving as the 'bridge' between the citizens and the metropolitan administration" (1989: 74). This open plaza functions more than a pit of a theatre which offers the citizens a chance to catch a glimpse of the officials working in the city hall buildings (Tajima 222).

8 The buildings were completed just three weeks before Suzuki's April election for his consecutive term as the governor, in which he was first time forced to run the campaign as an independent member of LDP. The New City Hall became the best promotion prop to the citizens in this competitive game of politics (Coaldrake 276). Also contradictory to the governor's statement of building a new city hall as a gift for the hard-working Tokyoites is the location of his office. Looking out to the Citizens' Plaza, his magnificent suite at the center of the twin buildings has an imperial style balcony, which "might foreseeably provide a spot for waving to a gathered populace against a monumental backdrop" (Tajima 224). Kenzo Tange, the patriarch architect of the postwar era, was responsible for the old metropolitan government office and the Tokyo Olympics Buildings. His open support of Suzuki's re-election, along with their old personal relationship before Suzuki's governor days, is considered one reason for his project for the New City Hall to be chosen over other competing ones.

9 In 1985, 60% commuters who work in three core wards spent more than 60 minutes to get to work, 20% of them spent 90 minutes (Udagawa 34).

10 See http://www.jarts.or.jp/en/tech/sec05.html.

11 Roman Cybriwsky, a scholar of Tokyo's urban landscape, gave two vivid examples to illustrate the unthinkably overcrowded subway train ride. He witnessed "a man who had been lifted out of one shoe by the press of the crowd, and who had the most awful time trying to retrieve it . . . " Another time a woman bumped her face against the man in front of her and left a clear lipstick mark on his white shirt (188). My own experience as a first-time tourist echoed a similar nightmare. I waited for half an hour to take the Chūō line, assuming the next train coming in 5 seconds might have room for me to squeeze in, only to find out that there will never be a train less crowded. Boosting all of my courage, I squeezed myself into the car. My body was twisted due to the compression. I was not standing on the ground of the train, but rather on a pile of feet. It was impossible to move an inch; therefore I wasn't able to see the name of the stop I was supposed to get off at. It didn't really make any difference since I was not able to move toward the door anyway.

Notes to Pages 80–100   **159**

CHAPTER 5

1. Homi Bhabha employs mimicry as the central trope in his theorization of colonial presence as a site of ambivalence. The colonial mimic man will not entirely resemble the colonizer but constitute a partial representation of the images, which the colonizer attempts to reconstruct in the colonized Other. Such a partial representation of the colonizer turns to be a subversive identity that questions the purity and originality of the authority. The mimic relationship between subject and abstract space is different from Bhabha's mimicry, which designates defiance against the environment, in that the former situation is an internal colonization. What confronts the occupant of abstract space is a power of no logo: the identity of the "colonizer" remains opaque.
2. *Tetsuo II: Body Hammer* and *Tokyo Fist*.
3. Tsukamoto's style is reminiscent of David Cronenberg and David Lynch, seasoned with the fascination of Godzilla series and Japanese video-game culture. The dominant background music is from laying the foundation of skyscrapers.
4. He is identified as "The Salaryman" in the credit.
5. The shots of Tsuda's routine walk in Tokyo suggest how mimesis successfully tames the subject: the salaryman follows the right pace of walking in the city and finds the right place in the society. The office scene in which the only thing Tsuda says to his superior with a polite bow "*onegaishimasu*" (please kindly…) reinforces the image of the indoctrinated body of the salaryman. In the space of corporate monumental, both the building as the material environment and the hierarchical corporate culture in the office offer models for Tsuda to imitate, the former a proud user of the capitalist space and the latter samurais, the feudal warriors devoted to the lords.
6. The color of the paint suggests blood.
7. The cryptic remarks can be a pertinent footnote to Tsuda's anger directed against the space. "It" is the power of the abstract space of Tokyo that has been determined Tsuda's life but never recognized as the rival.
8. Tsuda's survival despite the bleeding and severe wounds further illustrates the logic of masochism, which in essence "is not about death" but "nomadic disappearances," to disappear "like nomads in order to reappear somewhere else, where one is not expected" (Noyes 219). Tsuda's walking as a dysfunctional salaryman in the city exemplifies such a "nomadic disappearance" from the familiar social space.

PART THREE

1. The fast-paced development in Pudong is summarized by Shanghai officials as a maze to all: "The map will have to be changed once a week otherwise you'll

not be able to find your way about" (Xin 19). Such a statement might not be too much an exaggeration if we take a closer look at Shanghai's urban change as a whole since Pudong's development. According to Li Jianeng, Vice-President of the Pudong Development Office, the master plan is to revive Shanghai to become "the centre of the biggest economic and trading area in the West Pacific and we've chosen Pudong as the breakthrough point" (Lammie 174).

2 Under the Four Modernizations scheme, the open door policy was launched in 1978 (Olds 1995: 1729).

3 See Part Two for a detailed discussion of such kind of "mimesis" in Tokyo's case.

4 Shanghainese call *lilong*, their characteristic residential design, as *longtang*. "Long" means alley or lane and "tang" parlor or hall. "All houses are facing the lanes and lanes become the public space used by all residents. Enclosed, the whole *longtang* area seems to be a closed 'city within the city.' The bustling and noisy city is separated from the *longtang*. Once one enters the *longtang*, as if he had already been half at home" ("Life and Episodes in the Longtangs"). In the following discussion, *lilong* or *longtang* is sometimes referred to as alley houses.

CHAPTER 6

1 The report of the 14th Central Committee of CPC states, "We should also open more cities along the Yangtze River, while concentrating on the development and opening of the Pudong Area of Shanghai. We want to make Shanghai one of the international economic, financial and trade centers as soon as possible...." (Chen and Shi 14). The driving force of Shanghai and Pudong's economic rebound is Deng Xiaoping. During his visit in Shanghai in February 1990, Deng instructed to accelerate the development of Pudong (Cheung 78). For an analysis of the political context of Shanghai's development, see Peter T.Y. Chueng, who concluded that Shanghai's role as "China's most populous city, major cultural center and largest urban economy will ensure that it can never escape the watchful eyes of the central government, no matter who is in power" (82). Chueng's argument helps to explore the dynamics between state and global capital, which is more of a partnership than a zero-sum game. The timing of the announcement, several months after the Tiananmen massacre, is interpreted as "another success story to boost his [Deng Xiaoping's] stature and to strengthen his own political power in the aftermath of the 1989 political crisis" (Cheung 79). Such affirmation is also a reaffirmation of the open door policy after Tiananmen. For example, upon replying why Shanghai needs a fourth economic development zone in Pudong in addition to the three existing ones, then-mayor Zhu Rongji argues that Pudong as the largest development zone and the first bonded zone

"proves that Shanghai has the power and the superiority to further implement the policy of reform and opening to the outside world" ("Shanghai Mayor on Pudong Development"). Also see Thomas Gold's article for the politics of Pudong and Tiananmen.

2 The population of Pudong before 1990 is 1.33 million. Before 1992, Pudong was basically

> ... a large stretch of farmland with patches of desolate reed marshes. While Puxi (west of the Huangpu River) is the symbol of a flourishing metropolis, Pudong is the synonym of a rural village. Puxi and Pudong residents, divided by the river, seem like living in two different worlds. Therefore, a Shanghainese catchword is "rather have a bed in Puxi than a room in Pudong. " (Xin 18)

3 As a strategic city, "Shanghai has to make room for the global capital" (Wu 1374).

4 Pudong reminds one of the Lantau Island before Hong Kong government miraculously built Chek Lap Kok Airport and Disneyland on this quiet land as discussed in Part One.

5 For example, Fei Xiaotong, chairman of the China Democratic League, notes that Shanghai's Pudong should be developed as the future "mainland Hong Kong," "a centre of finance, foreign trade, information, transportation and science and technology" (27).

6 *Yongpan fengdian: Pudong kaifa kaifang shinian fazhan yanjiu chengguo jicui (Challenging the New Height: A Decade of Development of Pudong, Shanghai)* was an award-winning research project.

7 On the one hand, Pudong aspires to get closer to (靠攏) other global cities "physically" with the help of advanced technology and communications. To be connected with the global financial and commercial market is targeted from the very beginning as the primary function of Pudong. On a symbolic level, Pudong is expected to resemble as closely as possible these global cities on which it models.

8 Shanghai or Pudong is conceived as the dragon's head of the Yantzi River Valley. The dragon is a symbol of "China's future goal of becoming a global economic power" (Olds 1995: 1734).

9 For a careful discussion of the "global intelligence corps" and their works, see Kris Olds: "Globalizing Shanghai: the 'Global Intelligence Corps' and the Building of Pudong." Also see Streshinsky and Wu for the function of hiring these "foreign monks" as predominantly a marketing strategy to sell Pudong to the multinational consortia.

10 See *New and Trans-Century Architecture in Shanghai* Volume III, 120. By 2002, Pudong International Airport serves as the international airport of Shanghai, and Hongqiao Airport is mainly for domestic flights.
11 For an elaborate account of Shanghai's recent urban redevelopment and its social impact, see *Understanding Shanghai: From 1990 to 2000*.
12 By 1998, the total sum of import/export in Pudong is $11,982,000,000, 140% of the whole region's total net production (Yao 184).
13 As early as 1994, 45 world famous multinationals invested US$1,775 million in 57 projects in Pudong, 18.5% of the total FDI of US$9,580 million (Chen Shaoneng 3).
14 See Anthony G. O. Yeh for details of the preferential treatment to attract FDI.
15 For all the doubts cast upon building skyscrapers, a heatedly-debated issue in response to the September 11 attacks, Japanese construction company reassures the public that they will not be deterred by the terrorist threats. The project of the Global Financial Center in Shanghai is to be completed in time for Beijing Olympics in 2008. By that time, this building will be the tallest skyscraper in the world, currently the Twin Towers in Kuala Lumpur ("Shanghai Financial Center: Challenging the New Height").
16 The global compression, a force that demands an ever-expanding strategic space in the city for capital flows, drastically shrinks the urban space of the old city users, in particular, those who have no access to the spatial forms of global space.
17 As discussed in my previous chapters on Hong Kong, we see from the story of Hong Kong Disney such claims to the urban space, made by the power elite, as hotels, airports, and networks of inland transportation.
18 Olds summarizes Lujiazui Central Area Project as a coalition of the state and the global intelligence corps: "the design, construction, and marketing phases are being structured by the agents of contemporary globalization processes." In other words, Lujiazui is a space produced both "functionally and symbolically" for "the international firms which are charging into China in the 1990s" (1995: 1735).
19 For more details on the up-scale villa development, see Gaubatz "China's Urban Transformation: Patterns and Processes of Morphological Change in Beijing, Shanghai and Guangzhou."
20 Yu Minfei's observation on the land leases and rezoning supports Wu's argument:

> Land-leasing inevitably moves the inhabitants away from the city proper.... A brief survey of the 135 tracts of land transferred [in Shanghai between January and September 1992 — containing 818,000 square meters of housing] indicates that most of them are utilized for high-quality comprehensive buildings for

residence and offices for business. Because of this, many former residents have to be content with new houses in the suburbs, as few of them can move back into the city centre. Downtown Shanghai is becoming exclusively a commercial and financial centre. (qtd. in Gaubatz 1517)

The process of making space for the city to serve as a node of global capital is not unprecedented: in 1980s, for example, residents in Tokyo's CBD experienced a similar scenario.

CHAPTER 7

1. For the background of China's labor force and the control of the floating population, see Tamara Jacka's article "Wanted: Job for the Unwanted Migrant." Also see Li Peilin's *Transition in Social Stratification in the Market China* for detailed discussion of social classes in contemporary China.
2. According to Olds, the relocation was not a high-profiled issue for all the efforts of Kahn, a journalist who attempted to call attention to the relocation of residents in Shanghai (1995: 1737).
3. See Roger Chan's discussion on page 311.
4. Two recent books on the disappearing alley houses are *Shanghai Longtang Houses on the Verge of Disappearing* and *Shanghai Longtang*.
5. According to *New York Times* (May 30, 2001), Suzhou and Shanghai are the designated high-tech centers in China. As early as 1988, Shanghai's Caohejing Economic-Technological Development Zone was established to be the "Silicon Valley" of China. In 2000, IBM announced that they plan "to invest $300 million to build a chip-manufacturing plant in Shanghai, China" (Wilcox).
6. Pamela Yatsko tells the story of Ai Hua, a female worker who was laid off from a state-owned textile factory at the age of 38 after 17 years of hard work. The employer's story is that "our girls [lay-offs] can easily convert to being waitresses, stewardesses, subway personnel or neighbourhood committee workers." However, in Ai Hua's case, she was not qualified to take the training course provided by the factory after losing her job since she was not a member of the Communist Party. Her dream of being a maid for foreigners (service class) was shattered when she found out that she was too late to sign up for the highly competitive training program. A new job like a shop clerk is out of the picture. Ai Hua told the reporter: "The factory promised to find jobs for us in a short time. . . . So we're scared that if it calls and finds out we're already working, it will stop providing medical insurance and won't help us any more. If we lose the new job, then what?" (1996b: 59) As Yatsko argues, "Ai Hua is just one of the many Shanghai residents stuck in the city's past rather than its future" (1996b: 58).

7 The master plan drafted by the National Commission on Land Development of for Tokyo echoes Frankfurt, an emergent world city:

> From now to the coming 21st century, it is expected that Tokyo will acquire greater importance as a world city, by providing a basis for communication at both worldwide and national levels. To be effective in achieving these goals, Tokyo must resolve the functional paralysis caused by over-concentration, and make its living conditions more attractive. (qtd. in Machimura 1998: 183)

8 Lefebvre calls for the urgency to elucidate the deceptive transparency of space:

> The idea of a new life is at once realistic and illusory — and hence neither true nor false. What is true is that the preconditions for a different life have already been created, and that that other life is thus on the cards. What is false is the assumption that being on the cards and being imminent are the same thing, that what is immediately possible is necessarily a world away from what is only a distant possibility, or even an impossibility. The fact is that the space which contains the realized preconditions of another life is the same one as prohibits what those preconditions make possible. (189–90)

CHAPTER 8

1 To name a few: paradise of adventurers, whore of the orient, and the sin city.
2 For Benjamin's retelling the fairy tale of Sleeping Beauty, see Susan Buck-Morss's *The Dialectics of Seeing: Studies in Contemporary German Social Thought.*
3 Quotes from Wang's writings are my translation.
4 The novel was awarded the prestigious Mao Tun Literary Prize.
5 As Sasha describes, Wang Qiyao's cooking is homey but delicious (2000: 227).
6 Mrs. Yan considers her a friend for "remembering the good old days" because both of them have seen the good days of Shanghai and now take shelter at this less luxurious "Ping An Li."
7 Likewise, to Kang Mingxun, Wang Qiyao's lover and the father of her daughter, Wang's charms always have something to do with the old glory. She resembles the actress Ran Lingyu of the 1930s, the quintessential mystic enchantment of the time before Shanghai is liberated by communists: "He seems to see fanciful sights and sounds behind her, almost mirage-like" (2000: 203). The images of her photo, the magazine *Shanghai Life* and all the gossip about Miss Number

Three excite him:

> Now the city is a new one with all the roads renamed. The buildings and street lamps look the same, but the old interiors are gone. He remembers those days when even the wind felt romantic. . . . He feels that he moves along in time, but somehow forgets to take his heart with him from the previous generation and thus becomes a "heartless" man. It is Wang Qiyao, a reminder of the past that brings his heart back to him. (2000: 204)

Kang Mingxun is attracted to Wang Qiyao's charms that mirror the romantic Old Shanghai.

8. The narrator describes,

> Long Leg loves the crowd. It is these Shanghainese that make the city he loves. They are the masters of the beautiful streets, unlike he and his family, the looked-down-upon outsiders. Now with his hard work, he becomes one of them. Walking on the street, he feels like home. Every pedestrian is endeared as a family member, sharing the same thoughts with him. (2000: 361)

9. The disappeared laohuzao is displayed in the simulated street of the 1930s in Shanghai Urban Planning Exhibiton Hall.

Index

Abbas, Ackbar 18, 20, 46, 53, 54, 119, 150n9, 150n11, 150n14, 152n27, 153n5, 156n11
Abstract space 58, 59, 60, 63, 64, 65, 66, 69, 70, 71, 75, 77, 78, 79, 80, 81, 82, 83, 84, 87, 88, 89, 90, 92, 96, 97, 98, 102, 132, 136, 147n2, 159n1, 159n7
Alley house(s)/housing 6, 10, 102, 111, 114, 115, 120, 121, 122, 123, 124, 129, 134, 136, 160n4, 163n4
Appadurai, Arjun 4, 153n8
Arcade(s) 3, 50, 51, 53, 54, 151n22, 154n1
Asia's financial crises 156n11

Bank of China Tower 19, 20, 26, 33, 51, 150n10
Baudelaire, Charles 32, 153n9
Baudelairean *flâneur* 4, 8, 37, 41, 49, 50, 51, 55
Benjamin, Walter 7, 22, 38, 44, 50, 52, 55, 153n9, 153n12, 154n1, 155n5, 156n14, 164n2

Bhabha, Homi 80, 159n1
Blade Runner 51, 81, 83
Bubble (economy) 63, 66, 74, 155n11, 157n2
Buck-Morss, Susan 7, 8, 52, 164n2
Bund (Shanghai) 120

Caillois, Roger 60, 78, 79, 80
Calvino, Italo 14
Capital flow(s)/ Flow(s) of global capital/ Global capital flow(s) 2, 5, 6, 10, 16, 19, 24, 25, 32, 33, 41, 53, 63, 64, 65, 77, 103, 114, 116, 117, 136, 137, 147n2, 148n10, 149n6, 149n7, 155n11, 162n16
Capitalist space 6, 10, 11, 58, 59, 93, 96, 102, 109, 110, 117, 120, 159n5
Castells, Manuel 24
Causeway Bay (Hong Kong) 19
Central (Hong Kong) 18, 19, 20, 21, 24, 28, 33, 34, 37, 43, 50, 51, 53, 151n22, 155n9
Century Tower (Tokyo) 69, 70, 71, 74
Chek Lap Kok/International Airport 6,

168 Index

14, 22, 23, 106, 150n15, 151n23, 161n4
Chungking Express 3, 8, 14, 31-56
Chungking Mansion (Hong Kong) 34, 35, 50, 51, 53, 54, 153n6, 155n9
Cognitive mapping(s) 32, 49, 136, 152n1
Command-and-control cities/Command-post(s)/ Command-post city(cities) 5, 16, 18, 23, 116, 117, 148n7
Concrete space of everyday life 9, 59, 78, 125, 134, 135

de Certeau, Michel 4
Decentralization 5, 11
Decorporealization/ Decorporealized/ Decorporealizing 2, 70, 80, 93, 95, 97, 147n2
Deng, Xiaoping 160n1
Deterritorialization/Deterritorialized 2, 148n10
Dick, Philip 83
Disney/ Disney World/ Disneyland 6, 14, 15, 16, 17, 18, 20, 23, 75, 154n19, 156n12, 161n4, 162n17
Dual city 5, 6, 10, 26, 29, 55, 109, 130, 151n22
Dual compression 8, 14, 15, 31, 32, 37, 40, 44, 46, 50, 54

Everyday life 2, 3, 5, 6, 9, 10, 33, 43, 55, 59, 63, 64, 65, 69, 78, 84, 100, 101, 102, 110, 111, 113, 118, 120, 122, 123, 125, 126, 127, 128, 129, 130, 132, 133, 134, 135, 136, 137, 147n3, 148n9

Female *flâneur*/ Female walker 36, 44, 45
Flâneur(s) 4, 8, 14, 31, 32, 36, 37, 38, 39, 40, 41, 42, 43, 44, 45, 49, 50, 51, 52, 53, 55, 56, 126, 154n5, 155n9
Flexible accumulation 3, 10, 58, 64, 65, 69, 137
Foreign labor/Foreign laborer(s) 8, 35, 37, 55, 111, 112, 151n22
Foster, Norman 19, 70
Frankfurt 116, 117, 164n7
Freud, Sigmund 153n12, 154n13
Friedmann, John 5, 148n7

Gaze 32, 33, 34, 36, 37, 38, 39, 40, 41, 44, 45, 46, 49, 51, 52, 53, 55, 59, 70, 71, 89, 93, 95, 147n2
Giddens, Anthony 9
Girard, Réne 131
Global/local compression /Global and local compression 31, 34, 35, 46, 52
Global capital 2, 3, 4, 5, 6, 11, 14, 17, 19, 20, 23, 25, 28, 31, 36, 55, 64, 68, 69, 97, 108, 110, 116, 119, 132, 148n9, 148n10, 149n3, 152n25, 160n1, 161n3, 163n20
Global city (cities)/Global-city 1, 3, 4, 5, 6, 7, 8, 9, 10, 11, 14, 17, 18, 23, 27, 29, 31, 33, 34, 35, 36, 37, 38, 39, 41, 42, 44, 45, 46, 47, 52, 53, 54, 55, 56, 58, 59, 60, 63, 64, 65, 66, 67, 69, 70, 72, 73, 74, 76, 77, 81, 82, 88, 91, 92, 98, 100, 101, 102, 103, 104, 105, 106, 107, 108, 111, 112, 113, 116, 117, 118, 119, 120, 121, 129, 130, 132, 133, 134, 135, 136, 137, 138, 147n3, 147n4, 148n7, 148n8, 148n9, 149n1, 151n22, 155n11, 161n7

Global compression 8, 14, 16, 17, 18, 19, 20, 21, 22, 24, 26, 34, 35, 55, 149n6, 162n16
Global flow(s) 2, 3, 4, 6, 8, 16, 19, 20, 24, 29, 31, 34, 36, 46, 47, 52, 56, 60, 67, 69, 73, 98, 107, 111, 112, 137, 138, 148n10, 154n19
Global intelligence corps 105, 108, 113, 161n9, 162n18
Global space 9, 10, 22, 31, 32, 33, 34, 35, 36, 37, 38, 39, 41, 42, 43, 45, 46, 47, 49, 53, 54, 56, 59, 60, 63, 66, 69, 78, 109, 110, 113, 114, 115, 118, 119, 120, 136, 137, 148n9, 149n6, 156n13, 162n16
Globalization 1, 2, 3, 4, 5, 6, 7, 8, 9, 10, 14, 15, 16, 17, 21, 22, 23, 24, 25, 26, 27, 32, 36, 40, 45, 47, 49, 52, 53, 55, 56, 58, 60, 63, 65, 69, 70, 77, 87, 91, 92, 100, 101, 105, 107, 109, 110, 115, 117, 120, 121, 133, 135, 137, 138, 147n3, 147n5, 148n7, 148n10, 149n1, 155n9, 156n13, 156n14, 157n2, 162n18
Gregory, Derek 65, 147n2, 156n14

Handover (1997) 15, 23, 25, 149n1, 150n16, 151n24, 153n11, 155n11
Harvey, David 1, 5, 16, 17, 148n10, 148n11, 149n3, 149n4
Hongqiao Airport (Shanghai) 106, 162n10
HSBC Headquarters 19, 20, 26, 54, 70, 105, 151n22
Huangpu River (Shanghai) 100, 103, 113, 126, 161n2

Illegal immigrant(s)/Illegal immigration 26, 150n21, 151n23, 151n24
International business people 5, 6, 17, 21, 25, 108, 132
International division of labor 25

Jameson, Fredric 17, 46, 152n1
Jinmao Skyscraper 107

Kai Tak/Kai Tak Airport (Hong Kong) 22, 23, 34, 150n15, 153n4
King, Anthony D. 5, 148n7
Kowloon (Hong Kong) 22, 24, 135, 150n20

Lan Kwai Fong (Hong Kong) 20, 21, 22, 24, 43, 51, 53, 150n14
Lantau Island (Hong Kong) 6, 16, 22, 23, 28, 75, 149n2, 156n12, 161n4
Lefebvre, Henri 6, 7, 18, 19, 53, 58, 63, 64, 65, 66, 70, 71, 77, 79, 87, 89, 100, 118, 135, 148n9, 149n4, 157n1, 157n3, 157n5, 164n8
Leung, P.K. 21, 22, 24
Lilong(s) 10, 102, 115, 120, 121, 122, 123, 124, 126, 129, 130, 131, 132, 133, 134, 136, 160n4
Lived space 2, 3, 6, 10, 11, 17, 46, 52, 53, 59, 66, 69, 78, 79, 89, 93, 96, 101, 102, 107, 110, 111, 113, 114, 118, 121, 127, 132, 133, 136, 155n9
Local compression 8, 14, 24, 55
London 7, 9, 100, 103, 105, 107, 111
Longtang(s) 10, 121, 122, 123, 124, 126, 130, 132, 134, 160n4, 163n4
"Looking for Shanghai" 3, 133-6
Lujiazui (Shanghai) 100, 103, 104, 105, 107, 108, 113, 119, 162n18

Machimura, Takashi 116, 157n1, 157n2
"Meitou" 3, 120-1
Metonymy and metaphor 63, 157n3
Migrant(s)/Migrant laborer(s)/Migrant worker(s) 10, 25, 111, 112, 113, 130, 132, 136, 150n21
Mimesis 58, 59, 60, 63, 65, 66, 69, 71, 76, 77, 78, 81, 82, 84, 85, 87, 88, 90, 95, 97, 98, 131, 157n1, 159n5, 160n3
Mimicry 9, 60, 77, 78, 79, 80, 81, 82, 83, 86, 96, 97, 98, 159n1
Montage 7, 14, 43, 73, 95, 96, 101, 135, 136
Monumental building(s) 2, 18, 19, 20, 26, 51, 53, 70, 73, 74, 87, 107, 112, 137, 138, 147n3
Monumental space 1, 9, 10, 18, 19, 20, 24, 28, 29, 33, 36, 53, 54, 74, 101, 110, 133, 137
Monumentality 18, 150n12
Multinational/transnational consortia 8, 26, 36, 116, 161n9

New City Hall (Tokyo) 63, 69, 72, 73, 74, 92, 95, 157n5, 157n6, 157n7, 158n8
New Territories (Hong Kong) 28, 152n30, 155n9
New York 1, 7, 9, 100, 103, 104, 106, 107, 111, 148n5

Ohkawabashi River City 21 (Tokyo) 59, 69, 74, 75, 92, 157n3
Old Shanghai 10, 101, 102, 119, 120, 121, 122, 123, 125, 126, 127, 128, 129, 130, 131, 133, 134, 136, 165n7
Olds, Kris 105, 148n10, 161n9, 162n18, 163n2

Open door policy 100, 115, 160n2, 160n1
Open space 2, 3, 4, 8, 9, 11, 21, 24, 28, 42, 54, 84, 86, 94, 137, 138, 147n3, 151n22
Orient Pearl Television Tower (Shanghai) 107

Patten, Chris 22
Peripatetic school 3
Phantasmagoria 22, 156n14
Plato 58, 65, 157n1
Private space 32, 39, 45, 46, 53, 94, 148n9
Professional(s)/Professional managerial class/Top-level professional workers 8, 108, 109, 112, 147n4, 152n25
Public housing 14, 24, 26, 27, 28, 29, 53, 59, 69, 74, 75, 152n25, 152n26, 155n9
Public space 1, 7, 28, 134, 151n22, 160n4
Pudong (Shanghai) 6, 100, 101, 103, 104, 105, 106, 107, 108, 109, 112, 113, 119, 136, 159n1, 160n1, 161n2, 161n4, 161n5, 161n6, 161n7, 161n8, 161n9, 162n10, 162n12, 162n13
Pudong (International) Airport 106, 108, 162n10
Puxi (Shanghai) 104, 109, 113, 161n2

Relocation 6, 64, 66, 113, 114, 115, 116, 118, 136, 163n2
Representation of space 6, 8, 29, 49, 58, 135, 148n9, 155n7
Representational space 6, 7, 8, 29, 49, 58, 135, 148n9, 155n7
Rezoning 6, 10, 59, 64, 66, 69, 74, 113, 157n1, 162n20

Sassen, Saskia 5, 6, 17, 18, 29, 68, 107, 108, 147n4, 148n7, 148n10
Service class 42, 107, 108, 109, 110, 111, 112, 113, 116, 118, 132, 163n6
Shenzhen 152n24, 156n11
Shinjuku (Tokyo) 72, 74, 75, 92, 93, 158n7
Shock defense 40, 41, 44, 49, 51, 52
Shock experience 153n12
Simmel, Georg 44
Singapore 9, 104, 105, 106, 152n26, 156n11
Slum(s) 35, 36, 51, 53, 131
Social space 4, 8, 18, 29, 37, 38, 40, 91, 159n8
Song of Unending Sorrow 3, 120, 122-132

Tetsuo series 9, 60, 81, 86, 87
Tetsuo / Tetsuo: The Iron Man 3, 58, 80-83, 84
Tetsuo II: Body Hammer 3, 80, 81, 83-86, 92, 93, 159n2
Time-space compression 5, 10, 16, 17, 21, 41, 56, 147n2, 148n11
Tokyo Fist 3, 9, 58, 60, 80, 81, 86-98, 159n2
Tokyo Metropolitan Expressway 90, 91
Tsim Sha Tsui (Hong Kong) 24, 33, 34, 50, 51

Tsukamoto, Shinya 3, 7, 9, 58, 60, 80, 81, 86, 87, 92, 159n3

Uneven development 2, 6, 9, 10, 132

Victoria Harbor (Hong Kong) 24

Walk/Walking 1, 3, 4, 7, 8, 9, 11, 31, 32, 33, 34, 35, 36, 37, 38, 39, 40, 41, 42, 44, 45, 46, 52, 54, 55, 56, 58, 59, 60, 61, 74, 75, 77, 82, 83, 84, 85, 86, 87, 88, 89, 92, 94, 95, 97, 102, 121, 124, 126, 128, 129, 131, 133, 134, 135, 136, 138, 147n3, 153n6, 153n10, 155n9, 156n13, 159n4, 159n5, 159n8, 165n8
Wanchai (Hong Kong) 18, 19, 150n10
Wang, Anyi 3, 7, 10, 100, 101, 102, 119, 120, 121, 122, 123, 124, 125, 126, 129, 130, 131, 132, 133, 134, 135, 136
Wong, Kar-wai 3, 7, 8, 14, 31, 49-55, 153n6, 155n5, 155n6, 155n9, 155n10, 156n13
World city (cities)/world-city(cities) 5, 64, 66, 68, 72, 75, 100, 104, 105, 106, 112, 116 148n7, 164n7

Zhu, Rongji 105, 108, 160n1